'Round the world cooking library
Chinese Cooking

The secret of a great cuisine unveiled

Recipe contributions by Lee To Chun,
international authority on Chinese cooking

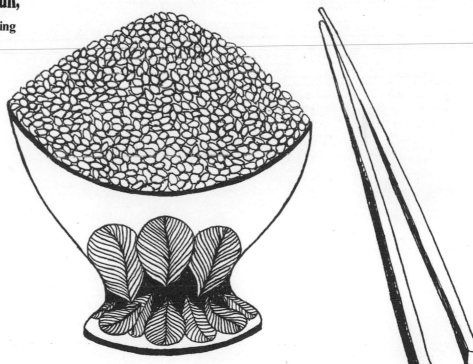

GARLAND BOOKS   NEW YORK

Contents

Recipe contributions	Lee To Chun, international authority on Chinese cooking and well known Hong-Kong-chef
American editor	Irena Kirshman, graduate Cordon Bleu Cooking School, lecturer on international cuisines, food consultant
Associate American editor	Susan Wright

Editorial staff for 'Round the world cooking library

Project editor	Ton van Es
Cover photo	Henk van der Heijden, Amsterdam
Text photos	Ed Suister, Amsterdam
Photos pp. 4, 5, 8, and 13 (ducks)	Sem Presser, Amsterdam
Photo p. 16	By courtesy of Rijksmuseum, Amsterdam
Design and drawings	Rosemarijn van Limburg Stirum, Amsterdam
Created by	Meijer Pers B.V., Amsterdam, The Netherlands
Typeset by	Service Type Inc., Lancaster, Pennsylvania and Internationaal Zetcentrum B.V., Wormerveer, The Netherlands
Printed by	Drukkerij Meijer B.V., Wormerveer, The Netherlands
Bound by	Proost en Brandt N.V., Amsterdam, The Netherlands
Publisher	Drake Publishers Inc., New York, N.Y.
Distributor	Garland Books, New York, N.Y.

Cup measures in this book are based on an eight ounce cup.

The art of Chinese Cooking

When you cook a Chinese meal you become part of the fascinating expression of the oldest enduring culture in the history of the world. No other people have exhibited such creativity, ingenuity, sense of taste and feeling for harmony in the preparation of their food. It is, therefore, both fitting and appropriate that Chinese cooking is described as an art. Yet even this definition is incomplete. Cooking and eating are so inextricably entwined that together they become not only an art, but also a recreation and a social activity for the Chinese people.

This culture of cooking and eating has developed methodically over a period of many generations. At a time when the rest of the ancient world was content to eat the results of a single fishing or hunting expedition, and the vegetables and fruits were only those which were found in a search of the immediate area, the Chinese were already deeply immersed in intricate culinary preparations. They were the first people to control the use of fire and to have a working conception of agriculture and crop rotation. They were able to cook their meats and select from a variety of vegetables. In fact they were so far along in their thinking that they were familiar with the use of certain roots and spices which, when added and cooked with the other ingredients, enhanced the final flavor of the dish. They even knew which particular combinations produced the most flavorful results. For the Chinese, food was not prepared merely to satisfy hunger, but also to provide a variety of esthetic pleasures.

Throughout her history, China has been essentially an agricultural country, and its people are still highly dependent on the results of each year's crops to save them from starvation. Yet in spite of the enormous land mass of China, only a relatively small part is arable. Year after year and season after season the Chinese have had to struggle to produce enough food on which to live. Crop failures and floods alternate with periods of drought and frequently there is a severe scarcity of food. To guard against natural disasters, the Chinese people developed techniques for preserving and storing food very early in their history.

The first method of keeping fish, vegetables and fruit was by drying them in the sun and the air. Later it was discovered that many foods could be pickled and preserved by packing them in salt. Occasionally both fresh and dried ingredients began to appear in the same dish, producing sophisticated contrasts of flavors as well as stretching a small quantity of a fresh ingredient to feed a larger number of people.

Because the quality of the soil is so poor in many regions of China, part of the inventiveness of the cooking can be attributed to necessity as much as to choice. The people were forced to find new sources of food to give some variety to their diet. The Chinese discovered that they could use many apparently unappetizing ingredients such as; roots and bulbs, fungi, seaweed, marine fauna and even flowers. Abalones, sea cucumber, lily roots, chrysanthemum leaves, sea weed, bamboo and water chestnuts and many, many other naturally growing foods are responsible for the unusual variety of interesting and exciting tastes in Chinese cooking

In order to get the greatest yield from a small plot of land, the farms were intensively cultivated to obtain the maximum production of vegetables or rice. The Chinese people could not afford to allow the fields to be given over for grazing cattle. Instead it was much more economical to use the animals for working the soil. The lack of grazing ground also explains the conspicuous absence of dairy products such as milk, cream, butter and cheese in the Chinese diet. Hogs, chickens and ducks were much easier to keep and considerably less demanding in their need for food. They would agreeably forage around the farmyard, scratching and rooting along the ditches to sustain themselves. Pork, because of its easy availability, thus holds a much more important place in the Chinese kitchen than beef.

Chickens and ducks are also used extensively in Chinese cooking for the same reason. The eggs were an added bonus without any extra work, at least on the part of the cook! If meat was eaten, it was always in small quantities. Vegetables and staple foods such as rice and grain had, and still have, the dominant role in Chinese cooking.

The Chinese people have had to cope not only with a scarcity of food, but also with a lack of fuel. This problem was solved with remarkable ingenuity. Just as they learned how to store food and obtain the maximum yield from each acre of land, they also found ways of extending the use of such heat as was available. They discovered, for example, that by boiling a chicken for a very short period of time, and then leaving it in its cooking liquid in a covered pot, it would continue to cook even when it was removed from the heat. Stir frying is the most fascinating method of cooking developed by the Chinese. In this method of cooking, all the ingredients are cut into small pieces and fried quickly in sizzling hot oil. The cooking time of each ingredient is arranged in such a way that, though the initial preparations may be fairly lengthy, the actual stir frying period normally does not exceed five minutes for any single dish.

Though even poor Chinese were able to eat relatively well with a minimum of resources, the most creative aspects and elements of fantasy in Chinese cooking were initiated by the wealthy people. The Imperial court and the well-to-do families

Setting out rice-plants.

Teaplants before the delicate top leaves are harvested.

constantly urged their cooks to create new dishes and new combinations of familiar ingredients, as well as to continue the search for fresh and exciting new delicacies. The sense of artistry and refinement found in Chinese calligraphy, poetry and pottery also appeared in the kitchen. New dishes were praised and exalted by such writers and poets as Confucius, Su Tung Po and many others who spread their own philosophies on the subjects of cooking and eating. This, in turn, also stimulated efforts to find new and different foods. One interesting dish, Tung Po pork, bears the name of the poet Su Tung Po. The names of other dishes such as Lion Head pork balls, Eight Jewel Fried Rice and many others, give an indication of the poetic and artistic acclaim with which these morsels were received.

The Chinese people do not use exaggerated garnishings on their food, but instead, allow each ingredient to play its own role in the composition of the dish. The peacock platter pictured on page 29 may prove that for the Chinese it is not enough to simply prepare a dish of cold meats to satisfy the appetite. Rather, each element becomes part of a general pattern; a harmonious range of contrasts in color, taste and texture, which taken together make the meal a complete experience. It is hardly surprising, after all the thought and effort which has

been expended in producing enough food and fuel for the evening meal, that the triumph should ultimately be shared with others. This is the time to relax, talk with friends and share the experiences of the day. The social aspects of a Chinese dinner are apparent in a restaurant as well as in the home. It is unthinkable for each person to order a meal according to his own preference and then devour it in solitary splendor! If a family or a group goes out to dine, the menu is carefully considered together and a number of dishes are ordered and served "family style" in common bowls to be enjoyed and sampled by everybody. Meeting a friend or relative on the street, the way to make inquiries about his state of well being is to ask: "has he eaten yet". If the friend comes to the house to visit, he is simply not allowed to leave without first being served a morsel of this or that or even a complete meal. Food is frequently given as a present, not only on special occasions such as the Chinese New Year and the feast of the Moon in August or September, but throughout the year as well. A toast is proposed to the good health of a friend by offering him a peach. The feast of the Moon is celebrated by the giving and receiving of a box containing four moon cakes, reflecting the phases of the moon.

If we keep in mind this idea of the family meal as an important

aspect of family life and consider the involvement of writers, poets and philosophers with good cooking and the pleasures of good food, then a direct comparison becomes apparent between Chinese cooking and the other great cuisines of the world. Certainly there are many things French and Chinese cooking have in common. In France many of the great chefs are also viewed as artists; in France too, the cooks have had the courage to experiment constantly in the search for new foods and new combinations of foods. In both

these great cuisines it is the simplicity of flavor and harmony of different ingredients which characterize the highest culinary achievements. The expression of Escoffier 'toujours faites simples' (always make it simple) could just as well have originated with a Chinese chef.

There are, however, salient differences between Chinese and Western cooking. Rice and noodles form the base of the Chinese diet and it is rare for the accent to be placed on one specific dish. (Peking duck is an exception to this rule.) Except at a Chinese banquet, the dishes

are not brought to the table one by one. Instead, they are all served together. Soup is not necessarily considered as the first course, but may be served at any time during the meal or even to conclude the dinner. In China, all the food is seasoned and cut into small pieces in the kitchen. The use of clanging, cold, clinical, metal knives, forks and spoons at the table reminds a Chinese person of a surgical operation rather than of gracious dining! The ingredients are cut into bite sized pieces by the cook so that they can be lifted easily from the bowl with

chopsticks. Vegetables, play a more important role than meat. Milk and milk products are almost completely absent. The Chinese do not serve a single sweet dessert. They offer an endless procession of snacks, savories and other goodies. Vegetable oils, particularly peanut oil, are used as the principal cooking agents. Lard is used occasionally, but butter is unknown in China. Wine is used extensively in Chinese cooking. Now let us move from generalities and look at each region of China more closely.

Regional Cooking

China is a vast country and has a climate ranging from tropical heat to extreme cold. The rainfall may be so heavy as to cause flooding, or so sparse that huge areas are actually desert land. The important difference between the food of the north and south of China lies in the staple foods. In the south, rice is the staple food, whereas in the north, rice is generally replaced with grain products like noodles and steamed bread. However, as a result of continuing migration and the fact that the Imperial court has changed its location from one city to another so many times, the differences between one area and another are far less noticeable nowadays. The recent cultural revolution also resulted in a narrowing of these differences. However, it is still possible to differentiate four areas which have made distinctive contributions to the national Chinese culinary art.

Canton and the southeast

Canton is the harbor city where the first contacts were made between the East and the West. To a certain extent it was at one time the most important of all Chinese cities, not only absorbing foreign influences from the West, but also in turn transmitting many aspects of the Chinese culture to the rest of the world. It is not surprising that the first Chinese restaurants which were established outside of China tended to follow the Cantonese style of cooking. The area around Canton has a rich and diverse culinary history. After the fall of the Ming dynasty in the 17th century, Canton welcomed the cooks who fled from the Imperial court. These cooks undoubtedly left their own distinctive marks on the cooking of their newly established home. Cantonese cooking is characterized by the use of very rich chicken broth. Few herbs and spices are used and little soy sauce is added in everyday cooking, though they appear from time to time to produce a little variation in the food. Bird's nests and sharks are prepared in a delicious way in this region. Sea food is abundant and plays an important role in the diet of the people. Canton lobster and Fu Yung Hai are typical examples of the Cantonese cooking. Crispy noodles, liquid filled roast duck, roast pork, fried rice, Siu Mai pork dumplings, deep fried and steamed dishes are all specialties which come from Canton and the surrounding area.

Peking and the north

Peking, situated near the great Chinese wall, is the old Imperial city of China. Until the 7th century the cooks of the Imperial court created the distinctive culinary art of this area. Honan, Shantung, Mongolia and Manchuria are also looked upon as sources of inspiration and influence. Grain is grown extensively in the northern part of China and noodles and steamed bread form the basis of the diet. Tales are told of the magnificent and gigantic banquets of Peking. Famous feasts composed of hundreds of dishes were served in unending procession. The onion family; onion garlic, and scallions are all popular and widely used in northern cooking. The influences of the Muslims and nomadic tribes are apparent, for instance, in the use of lamb in the north. It is rarely, if ever encountered throughout the rest of China. Lamb, and occasionally other meats, are broiled over charcoal, and hot-pot cooking originated here. Typical of these hot-pot dishes is the recipe for Ta Pin Lo. Many foods are steamed or clear simmered, a cooking method in which the dish retains its pure, natural flavor. These are techniques which distinguish the cooking of the north. Many sweet sour dishes, especially sweet sour fish, come from this area. The cooking typically has a light and delicate touch and a considerable amount of wine is used in the preparation of the northern food. The following dishes are well known as being typical of northern Chinese cooking: Steamed Buns, Peking duck, Peking doilies, Tung Po pork, carp preparations from the Hoang-Ho (the Yellow river), light dishes such as Chicken Velvet, cold meat in jelly, egg rolls and their predecessors spring rolls and desserts such as Peking dust and apple fritters.

Szechuan and the west

The most distinctive aspect of the Szechuan school is the widespread use of Szechuan pepper. Relatively strongly spiced and peppered dishes are typical of the region. The area surrounding Yunan is famous for its ham; and twice cooked pork is one example of the many cooking techniques known to have originated here. Nuts, cloud-ear mushrooms, chicken, hot peppers and chicken fat are all popular ingredients in the west. Szechuan duck is one of the most famous of the specialities. In this famous preparation, the duck is first steamed and then deep fried. Another famous dish, deep fried, paper-wrapped chicken, is also popular in Szechuan.

Fukien and the northeastern coast provinces

Fish and the sea food gathered from the great rivers and the sea are natural favorites of this area, though the importance of soups is its most remarkable culinary characteristic. Soups come in many varieties and it is quite common to serve two or even more soups at any given meal. Most of them are clear soups. The quality of the soy sauce is superior and red cooked dishes also distinguish this area. Soft stuffed pancakes and giant shrimp are typical specialities, and Shanghai boasts of the quality of its bird's nest soup. A noticeably, sweet red seasoning is made from wine sediment and fermented rice. Suckling pig and pork knuckles are famous Shanghai dishes.

Cooking techniques

For centuries the Chinese have learned to live on small scraps yet eat well.

The techniques used in Chinese cooking are often completely different from those used in the preparation of food in the West. Ovens are rarely seen in a private household. Only restaurants have ovens to roast large cuts of meat and certain specialty dishes such as Peking duck. These foods are then bought by weight by the family, and are completely, or at least partially, cooked.

Stir frying

This is by far the most original method of cooking which has been developed by the Chinese people. It is a logical, efficient and practical solution to the problem of the scarcity of fuel. The food is cooked quickly over high heat in a bowl-like metal pan called a "wok". None of the nutrients are lost in the cooking process and so the food not only looks and tastes good, but is nutritionally sound too. Meat, poultry, seafood and vegetables can all be cooked in this manner.

The basic principles of stir-fry cooking are: first, that the ingredients are cut into small pieces before they are cooked. They are then fried in a little oil as quickly as possible at a very high temperature. During the actual cooking the pieces of food are stirred, scooped and turned over and over as quickly as possible inside the oiled wok. The outer surface of each ingredient comes briefly, but frequently, into contact with the hot surface of the metal just long enough for it to be

almost completely cooked through. There is no loss of color, flavor or juices and each piece of food retains its own natural characteristics. After the initial frying, hot broth is added to the pan. The heat is reduced and the ingredients, often in a covered pan, are cooked for a few minutes longer until they are quite tender but still crisp. The broth is usually thickened by adding cornstarch dissolved in cold water. The dish is then served immediately. The whole cooking process takes only a few minutes and some ingredients require no more than a few seconds of cooking.

Because the cooking time is so short, it is of the utmost importance that all the initial preparation must be done in advance, and everything is organized down to the last detail before the actual cooking begins. The ingredients to be cut, soaked or parboiled must all be ready at hand and arranged in the correct sequence so that they can be added at the right moment. Parboiling and soaking must be done before the actual cooking starts. As soon as the heat is on, literally not a second can be lost looking for a missing ingredient or rereading the recipe. This is why it is a good idea to read over the recipe for stir fried dishes two or three times so you are really sure that you know the order in which the ingredients are to be added. Though the recipe may at first seem rather complicated it generally involves

only a few simple steps, and you will find yourself getting quicker and quicker. As long as you remember that foods such as meat will require more cooking than bean sprouts, the sequence seems quite sensible and reasonable and won't appear to be nearly as mysterious.

Precise cooking times have been given for all the stir frying recipes but, as you can imagine, it is absolutely impossible to be completely dogmatic in prescribing cooking times for all cooking methods. If, for example, a dish requires two hours simmering time, five minutes more or less will make very little difference. However, the reason for timing the stir fried dishes so accurately is that half a minute of extra cooking will make a considerable difference. Be sure to taste the

food if you are in any doubt and see if it is ready before removing it from the heat. Bear in mind though, that the longer the dish is stir fried, the greater will be the loss of color, taste and texture. Slight variations in cooking times, even in stir frying, are bound to occur and depend largely on the temperature of the burner, the thickness of the pan, the quality and freshness of the ingredients and the temperature of the broth which is added.

In the final analysis the judgement and experience of the cook must determine the ultimate excellence of the dish. Fry just long enough for a complete change of color. Fish will become white and opaque. Pork and chicken are done when they have turned from pink to white. Beef is ready when it has lost any trace of redness and is a

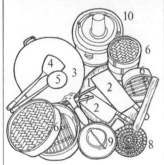

*Some typical Chinese
cooking-utensils:*
1 Chopping block
2 Cleavers
3 Wok
4 Wok-chan spatula
5 Siou-hok ladle
6 Bamboo-steamers
7 Chopsticks
8 Deepfrying strainer
9 Nga Po-casserole dish
10 Ta Pin Lo or Hot pot

pale, uniform brown color. Green vegetables are done sufficiently when a deep, clear, fresh color appears. While keeping an eye on the ingredients which are cooking, try to think of the next step in the preparation of the dish. The cooking will then flow easily and without any frenzy or worry. Having created a masterpiece, it goes without saying that it should be served immediately and not be reheated. Guests have to wait for the dish, not the other way around. Stir frying always has to be a last minute method of cooking. Always begin by heating the pan to be sure it is completely dry and hot before adding the oil. Add the oil in a circular motion to coat the sides evenly. The oil should be hot but not sizzling. Usually salt, garlic and ginger root are added to flavor the oil, then the meat, the vegetables and the broth are added. Finally the liquid is thickened into a sauce by adding cornstarch dissolved in cold water. The order in which the ingredients are added may vary from time to time, depending on a particular recipe. If it seems that there is insufficient oil in the pan, and the ingredients are sticking to the sides, then add a little more oil. Be sure to allow the new oil to become very hot before it comes into contact with the food which is cooking by introducing it in a circular motion over the high sloping sides of the pan. Garlic and ginger, particularly garlic, are often removed before the

remaining ingredients are added. It is important, especially with meat, not to fry too large a quantity at one time. For example, not more than a pound of meat should be added all at once or the temperature of the oil will be reduced so much that the meat will steam rather than fry. It is better to cook the meat in two batches. Various ingredients require different amounts of heat. Vegetables and fish will require less cooking time than meat, and both must be turned more carefully than meat or they will fall apart. Bean sprouts and bean curd are particularly fragile and must be handled very carefully. Bean curd and fish should be turned rather than actually stirred like the other ingredients. The quantity of broth which is added depends largely on the firmness of the vegetables. Firm vegetables such as carrots contain less liquid of their own and require rather more liquid to complete their cooking than a soft leafy green vegetable, such as spinach, which produces a certain amount of liquid itself as it cooks. The cornstarch mixture thickens the liquid into a clear transparent sauce to coat all the ingredients and unify them into a complete dish. It is generally a good plan for a beginner to cook only one stir fried dish at each meal and complete the menu with braised or steamed dishes. Attempting to juggle with two or more stir fried dishes the first time becomes rather complicated and almost invariably results

in great disappointment.

Steaming

Steaming is a method of cooking which is used very frequently in China, and almost all ingredients including meats, chicken, fish, vegetables, eggs, dumplings, rice and even cakes can be steamed successfully. Foods such as dumplings, meat or fish balls are best placed on a foil or wax paper covered rack to prevent them from sticking. Fish is steamed in a shallow dish, and meats and chicken are generally placed in a bowl. The purpose of steaming is to retain the pure, natural flavor and color of the food. When the food is steamed in a bowl, the container is placed in a larger pan, and boiling water is added until it comes two thirds of the way up the outer side of the bowl. Foods steamed on a rack or a shallow dish are suspended above the boiling water in a special steamer. Three or four inches of water should be kept at a low boil to produce enough steam to cook the food. The level of the water can be maintained by adding more boiling water from time to time. The heat should be regulated to prevent the water from boiling away too rapidly thus making it necessary to raise the lid and interrupt the steaming process. Be sure that a plate or bowl really is heatproof before using it for steaming. The pan must always be covered with a tight fitting lid or too much steam will escape.

Deep frying

There are a few ways in which the Chinese method of deep frying differs from the Western way. Chinese deep frying is generally completed in two stages. First the ingredients are lightly colored in hot oil. They are then removed from the pan, and, during the time which it takes for the oil to become very hot again, the drained ingredients are allowed to cool on the outside. The food is then fried a second time until it is golden brown and crisp on the outside and soft and tender on the inside. Occasionally the ingredients are fried only once, providing the temperature is lowered after they are added and then raised until the oil is very hot just before the cooking time has been completed. Most ingredients which are to be deep fried are cut into medium sized pieces though sometimes both fish and chicken are fried whole. Chicken and duck are often initially steamed to remove the fat from the skin, then dried and finally deep fried. The ingredients are usually dredged in flour or cornstarch, or dipped in a batter to seal the food. This prevents any loss of the delicate juices and makes the outside even more crisp. Many foods are marinated before being deep fried.

The wok

The wok, or 'cooking vessel' as the Chinese call it, is one of the most perfectly designed utensils ever invented. It is a section of a globe with a round bottom and wide flaring sides. The best woks are made from thin, tempered iron which allows the heat to be conducted evenly. They were originally made to be set over the round opening of a furnace or stove, or balanced between three stones over an open fire. The wide flaring sides of the wok conduct the heat evenly and rapidly to make an extremely large cooking surface. In coping with a chronic fuel shortage this was an important advantage in China. However, the round bottom is not practical in a Western kitchen and it needs a special metal ring to stabilize it over the gas or electric burner. These metal rings can be bought in any shop that sells woks. A specially designed lid, usually made of aluminum and shaped like a flattened cone with inward sloping sides, can be bought to go with the wok in most shops. The particular design makes the wok a highly versatile utensil. It is ideal for stir frying because there are no actual sides and bottom. The sides of the wok are as hot as the bottom, the food can be moved around and around and stirred over and over without ever losing contact with the source of heat and food is not easily spilled. It is light and easy to handle and, because of its thinness, the distribution of the heat can be regulated very quickly and very precisely. It is equally perfect for making omelets or for use with a steamer (described further on). Considerably less oil is needed when deep frying in a wok than in a conventional skillet. In fact the wok can be used for almost every cooking technique employed in Chinese cooking. The ideal size for a wok is fourteen to fifteen inches across the top. This size is easy to manage and holds almost all the dishes you are likely to be cooking. For braising and red simmering a heavier pot or casserole is sometimes preferable. The wok is extremely useful for stir frying and steaming, in combination with a set of bamboo steaming baskets. When you buy a new wok it must be seasoned in a special way. First wash it with a detergent, then rinse and dry it thoroughly over a low heat. Add two tablespoons of peanut oil. Heat the oil until it starts to smoke, then tilt the pan in all directions to coat the sides evenly. Take it off the heat, pour out the excess oil, rinse it again with hot water and then dry it. Repeat this procedure once. Dry the wok and add one tablespoon of oil. Rub the oil around the inside with a paper towel. After this initial cleaning, do not ever wash the wok again with a detergent. Just rinse it out with water and rub it with a sponge or soft brush. Dry it with a clean cloth and invert it over the heat to dry it completely. If any food is still sticking to the pan, add a little oil and some salt and scour it away with a paper towel. In time, the wok will turn black with use. A well blackened wok will be a sign of distinction in your kitchen. If you do not have a wok, a twelve to fourteen inch skillet with high flaring sides can be used instead. If certain ingredients have to be cooked in a specific way, other utensil substitutions will be described in the particular recipe.

Wok chan and siou hok

A wok chan is a spatula which is used in combination with a siou hok (a Chinese ladle) in the preparation of stir fried dishes. The spatula has a blade with a slightly rounded surface that slides easily along the curved sides of the wok. These handmade utensils are made of iron and sometimes have a chrome finish. They are inexpensive and a great joy to work with.

The cleaver

The Chinese cleaver knife is a large, heavy, razor sharp tool. Watching a Chinese chef work with this seemingly awkward knife is like watching a fascinating and breathtaking circus act. He works with dazzling speed and astonishing accuracy, cutting, chopping and slicing the ingredients. The flat side of the cleaver is used for crushing garlic and carrying the prepared ingredients from the chopping block into the wok. Even the end of the wooden handle can be used as a pestle to crush or mash peppercorns or black beans. Chinese cleavers can be bought in a variety of sizes. The blade is generally between seven to ten inches in length and the height may be between three and seven inches. The four or five inch handle of the cleaver is generally just the right size to be held most comfortably. Some blades are made with a curved edge but the straight bladed knives are found in the stores more easily and are the most practical. When buying a cleaver, choose a heavy one. Though it may seem difficult to manipulate at first, you will soon get used to it and begin to regard it as a trusted friend. The blade of the cleaver may be made from carbon or stainless steel. Carbon steel is the best choice as it will hold a sharper edge, though it will rust if it is not handled properly. Always rinse it after cutting onions or lemons, dry it thoroughly and store it in a dry place. If you do not have a cleaver use a large heavy chef's knife. Like a cleaver, it should be kept razor sharp and carbon steel is again a better choice than stainless steel.

The Chinese chopping block

The Chinese chopping block (see picture) is the perfect partner for the cleaver. It is simply a horizontal piece of tropical tree which has been slightly polished. These chopping blocks are generally fifteen to twenty five inches in diameter. The thickness of the block is even more important than the diameter. It should be at least four inches thick, and preferably six to eight inches. Be sure to choose a heavy, thick block that will not slip when you use it. The block should first be soaked in salted water, then wiped dry and rubbed with oil. As it is very handy for all cutting purposes, it can be used every day. Constant use will also prevent the block from drying out and getting large cracks in it. If it does become dry, you can place it in a sink, cover it with water and put a heavy object on it to prevent it from floating. When it is not in use, it is best to keep it standing on its side. If it is kept lying flat, mould might form on the under side. If a block is not available, a heavy cutting board can be used instead.

Chop sticks

Chop sticks (see picture) are used both for preparing and eating the food. The ones used for cooking are usually a few inches longer than those used for eating. They should preferably be made of wood or bamboo. Depending on what is to be done with them, they can be used singly or in pairs. Chop sticks can be used for beating eggs, stirring and many other kitchen procedures. (Chop sticks used for eating the food and a description of how to use them can be found under a separate heading.)

Wire ladle

A shallow wire ladle (see picture) with a bamboo handle is used for deep frying. Though it is not an absolutely essential piece of equipment, it functions very well and drains the fat from the food quickly. Though a Chinese wire ladle is extremely nice to look at, it can easily be replaced with any wire basket, strainer or even a slotted spoon.

Bamboo Steamer

The Chinese use rounded steaming baskets (see picture) made of bamboo, with a woven bamboo lid. The baskets can be stacked one on top of the other in such a way that many different foods can be steamed simultaneously in the same pan. The bottom is a sort of bamboo lattice work which permits the steam to enter. If several foods have to be steamed at one time, or if many small items have to be steamed, you simply fill each layer with a number of these things, put the layers on top of each other, cover with the bamboo lid and place the whole stack in a wok filled with three or four inches of boiling water. Steaming can also be done in other steaming pans (mostly made of aluminum). Even if you do not have a special steaming device, you can easily improvise one. Place a rack or shallow bowl in a pan. (Or in an emergency use an inverted cup, bowl or even a can with the top and bottom removed.) A few inches of water are brought to

Rice and noodles are the staple starches of the Chinese diet.

a boil in a pan wide enough to permit the steam to circulate between the sides of the bowl and the sides of the pan. The rack or bowl containing the food is placed on the supporting device in such a way that it is suspended at least one inch above the boiling water.

Ta Pin Lo

A Ta Pin Lo, or Mongolian Fire pot, is a hot-pot which consists of a basin formed around a cone shaped chimney-like funnel. The basin is situated halfway down the funnel. Charcoal or methylated spirits are usually used in the bottom part to furnish the heat. The pan can be covered with a lid which has a hole in the center through which the lid is fitted over the funnel. The basin is filled with chicken or meat broth which is brought to a boil and various ingredients are cooked in this broth at the table. A recipe for such a dinner can be found on page 90. This Ta Pin Lo is a very good looking, but rather expensive conversation piece, and it can be replaced by either a large electric frying pan, a saucepan which can be used on top of a spirit burner, an indoor grill or an electric hot plate. For simmered dishes, a heavy metal or earthenware casserole with a tight-fitting lid can be used. To ensure really slow cooking, an asbestos pad may be used under the casserole. A deep pan, preferably made of a material that conducts the heat evenly, such as tin lined copper or heavy duty aluminum,

is the best choice for cooking rice. Experience is invaluable in cooking perfect rice every time. The results are strongly determined by the balance between the rice, the water and the correct amount of heat. A good saucepan, a rolling pin, a board, a strainer, a few bowls and measuring spoons are all you need to complete the equipment for entering the world of Chinese cooking. Once again, let us emphasize that Chinese cooking can be done very successfully without one single piece of special Chinese equipment. These tools only add to the efficiency of your kitchen and can also be used in Western cooking. They also give the extra satisfaction of working with utensils that are designed specially for the job. The preparation and the cutting of the ingredients are of the utmost importance in Chinese cooking. The initial preparation of a dish generally takes relatively much longer than the cooking time. This is particularly true with stir frying. Because of the scarcity of fuel in China, the food is almost always cut into small pieces. It is then possible to get the best results from the heat that is available. In order to cook a whole chicken, it takes at least twenty to thirty minutes, but the same chicken, when cut into small pieces, can be cooked in a matter of five or six minutes. This is because the heat can penetrate small pieces of food more rapidly, and the cooking surface is particularly large in

The four main flavorings in Chinese cooking are soy sauce, rice wine (or sherry), ginger and garlic.

Roast ducks can be bought by weight in Chinese street stalls.

The Chinese use a special oven for Peking Duck.

relation to the volume. One of the reasons that carrots are often cut into strange irregular forms is to expose as large a surface as possible to the heat of the pan. The manner in which an ingredient is to be cooked determines the way in which it is to be cut. The method of cutting is also important from an esthetic point of view. Formless bits and pieces are like thorns in the flesh of the Chinese. The ingredients must not only go well together as far as flavor, color and texture are concerned, but they must be in proportionately harmonious forms. Cutting makes up a very important part of a cook's education in China and it frequently happens that several months or even a year is spent learning and practicing how to cut. Only after he has learned to handle a cleaver like a master and after he can cut a chicken in neat pieces, attacking the bird in exactly the right spots, can he go on to real cooking. The Chinese cook always uses a heavy, sharp cleaver instead of a knife. He not only uses the sharp edge but also the blunt top side, and the flat side of the blade as well as the handle. The best way to hold the cleaver is to let the handle rest in your three last fingers and to guide the blade by laying your thumb

and index finger along the upper side. Place the knife with its edge firmly on the chopping block and remember that the food, and not the knife, moves. The point of the knife remains on the chopping block, the back end of the blade is slightly raised and the food is pushed through underneath with the left hand. Put the ingredients that are to be cut in the correct cutting direction at a 90° angle against the blade. Meat, for example, should be cut across the grain. Fold the thumb of your left hand across your palm, fold your fingers over so that if you put your hand on the table it rests on the joints. Put your clenched hand in the proper direction on the food with your knuckles against the blade of the knife. For example, if you have to cut ingredients into half inch pieces, pull your left hand back half an inch. Lift the knife so that the ingredients can just go under it. Push the ingredients forward until your knuckles rest again against the wide blade of the knife. Let the knife come down and the first piece is cut. In the beginning it is probably easier to let the knife move forward slightly so that the cutting movement will be neater, although an up-and-down movement will eventually prove to be faster and easier. Do not use excessive strength. The weight of the knife in combination with its sharpness is usually sufficient to do the cutting. There is no danger of cutting yourself if you never lift the knife higher than your knuckles. Only when you are cutting chicken with the bone in is it necessary to lift the knife higher in order to get the required power. In that case, keep your fingers well out of the way! Keeping the knife razor sharp is important not only because it makes working with it easier, but also because the ingredients become bruised with a blunt knife. If you do not have a Chinese cleaver knife, use a large, sturdy chef's knife with a wedge-shaped blade. Hold the handle with the fingers of your right hand and hold the tip of the blade down on the chopping block with the fingers of your left hand when you have to mince or chop ingredients finely.

The Chinese cut in the following ways:

Straight slicing:
The knife is held and moved as described above and the food is cut at a right angle. This method of cutting is used for many foods, particularly ingredients like meats, fish and soft vegetables.

Diagonal slicing:
With this method, the knife and the ingredient being cut form a 45° horizontal angle to each other. The cutting is usually not done vertically, but with the blade leaning slightly inward. This method is used with cylindrical, fibrous, tough and stalky vegetables and coarser meats. The idea is to expose as large an area as possible to the source of heat and thus speed up the cooking process.

Diagonal rolling cut:
This method is used almost exclusively with cylindrical, firm ingredients like carrots, asparagus, turnips, etc. It is done about the same way as with diagonal slicing but after the first slice, the ingredient is rolled towards the knife so that the second cut is made partly through the surface exposed by the previous cut. The angle at which the ingredient is cut is even smaller, about 30°–40° which results in long, pointed, irregularly shaped pieces with a maximum cooking surface.

Shredding:
With this method the knife is held at a right angle to the cutting board again, and the ingredients are first cut into thin slices and then the slices are cut lengthwise into shreds; usually not longer than about 2½ inches and not shorter than about 1 inch. Depending on their use, they can be as thick as a match stick (such as bamboo used in soups), or as fine as threads (such as egg garnish).

Dicing:
Ingredients are first sliced and then cut into strips, or cut directly into strips. These strips are cut crosswise into cubes which, depending on the ingredient and the way in which it is to be used, will vary from about ½ inch to 1 inch.

Mincing:
Mincing is done with the extreme tip of the knife steadied on the chopping block with the left hand. The blade is moved up and down quickly in a fan-like circular movement with the tip of the knife as the centerpoint. Then the process is repeated in another direction until the food is very finely minced. In between changes in direction, the pieces are swept into a pile with the blade and the chopping begins again. Both a meat grinder and a blender could be used, but too many juices are lost and the ingredients are bruised and mashed to a pulp.

Slow cooking methods
Slow cooking includes a number of similar techniques employed for the purpose of cooking the food very slowly over low heat. Generally a fairly large piece of meat or chicken is placed in a heavy pan or casserole with a tight fitting lid. The cooking is done on top of the stove rather than in the oven. If it is available, an asbestos mat, placed under the casserole will allow an even slower cooking process.

Braising
With this technique, the ingredients are first plunged into hot oil or water to seal in the juices and they are then cooked slowly over low heat in a heavy, covered pan to which some liquid has been added. Ingredients are mostly left whole, though they can be cut up. This is a favorite technique for cooking young tender poultry, meat, fish and vegetables like turnips, etc. Usually the ingredients are not turned during cooking.

Red simmering
This is a process of stewing to produce a rich reddish brown gravy. It is this gravy that gives the method its name. Red simmering generally takes more time than braising. Pork, beef, poultry and, in the North of China, lamb are all prepared in this way. The piece of meat is generally cooked whole, then cut into slices or cubes after it has been cooked completely, though occasionally the meat is cut up first to speed the cooking time. Along with the soy sauce that gives the sauce its attractive color and taste, seasonings such as star anise, cinnamon, five spice powder, ginger, sugar and sherry are often added. The meat is turned several times in the sauce.

Red simmered dishes can be served hot or cold. When served cold, the gravy turns into a delicious jelly. The gravy can also be used on its own as a sauce over rice or other dishes. Only a small portion is served with the meat and the rest is often used as a starter for the so-called Master sauce (see recipe page 82). This sauce is used over and over again to cook red simmered dishes. It is replenished and freshened from time to time with broth, soy sauce, sherry and other flavorings. Red simmered dishes can be made well in advance. They can be kept for several days under refrigeration and the flavor improves when the dish is reheated. Fresh or dried vegetables can also be added to improve the flavor.

White simmering
In white simmered dishes, the

soy sauce and highly aromatic flavorings are left out and usually only sherry, ginger and scallions are added for flavor. The purpose of this method, which is used for cooking poultry, pork and fish, is to obtain a rich, pure, natural flavor. Vegetables are frequently added to the meats and the broth is eaten as a soup. The natural, bland taste of these dishes is often complemented by accompanying dip sauces served on the table.

White simmering, also called clear simmering, includes some other interesting ways of preparing meats, poultry or fish. In one of them, the food, often a tender young chicken, is cooked briefly over medium heat. Then the heat is turned off and the meat is left to cool in the broth. The heat of the broth completes the cooking. On and off cookery is also included under the heading of white simmering. With this method, the heat is turned on and off several times during cooking.

Roasting

Poultry and pork are the only meats which are roasted in China. Originally roasting was only done in ovens, but charcoal grills are also being used nowadays. However, roasting is still most successfully done in an oven. The meat is either hung from hooks, placed on a rack or turned on a spit. The meat is often marinated first, then rubbed with oil and basted frequently with seasonings during the roasting time.

Chicken or duck may be seasoned inside or even be filled with liquid (see Cantonese duck, recipe page 50). Hanging the meat from freely rotating hooks is the best method of roasting it evenly. A pan with some water is placed under the meat to catch the drippings. As an oven is not a very common thing in the Chinese household, roast meats and poultry are generally sold by weight in restaurants and shops. Roast meat, especially pork, is used as an ingredient in quite a number of dishes.

Parboiling and blanching

In Chinese cooking, parboiling is mostly used to soften tougher vegetables such as broccoli and carrots to prepare them for brief cooking techniques like stir frying or as soup ingredients. The ingredients are cooked briefly in rapidly boiling water, then rinsed under cold running water. In this way, they retain their crispness and bright color. Sometimes parboiling is done to remove an unwanted strong taste such as in bitter melon or, in the case of polutry, to remove the fat from the skin or to seal in the juices.

In blanching, boiling water is poured over the ingredients which are then either left in this water for a short time or drained immediately. Bean sprouts are usually treated this way.

In Chinese cooking, several techniques are often combined. For example, duck may be first roasted, then cut into pieces and finally stir fried (see stir fried roast duck, recipe page 51), or chicken may be first steamed and then stir fried.

Other techniques

Pan frying is a technique used sometimes for cooking omelettes and fish. The ingredients are cooked over medium heat and, unlike stir frying, are handled as little as possible.

Poaching is the method used for cooking delicate foods such as fish, shrimp balls, chicken velvet etc. It is a short process in which the liquid is not allowed to come to a rolling boil, but instead is kept at a simmering point. Broth is often used instead of water.

Chopsticks

Chinese tea and wine are the best accompaniments to Chinese food.

Blue and white China pouring-vessel with cover in the shape of twin mandarin-ducks, symbolizing conjugal felicity. Ming-dynasty, late 16th century.

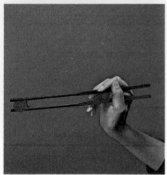

Place one chopstick in the right hand, held by the base of the thumb and the top of the ringfinger, fingers slightly bent. The second chopstick is held by the top of the thumb and the tops of the middle- and indexfinger. The first chopstick remains stationary while the second one is moved up and down by the middle- and indexfinger, the thumb remaining in almost the same position.

Chopsticks are used both in cooking and eating the food. Those used for cooking are usually longer than the ones for eating. For cooking, the wooden or bamboo chopsticks are used almost exclusively because those made of other materials such as plastic, ivory, or precious metal, either conduct too much heat or are ruined by the heat. In cooking, chopsticks are easy to manipulate in a wok and are used for stirring or to remove small pieces of food such as garlic or ginger root. The chopsticks used to eat the food are sometime made of ivory, and though these are particularly beautiful, they have the disadvantage of needing to be treated very carefully and not exposed to extreme heat or they will crack. Unfortunately, ivory chopsticks also tend to discolor over a period of time. Chopsticks made of wood or bamboo are quite satisfactory, and even plastic ones can be used in an emergency. Apart from the fact that metal knives, forks and spoons impart a slightly metallic flavor to the food, chopsticks have the additional advantage that the ones made of wood or bamboo do not conduct heat, so there is less danger of a burned tongue! It will seem rather awkward to hold the chopsticks in the correct position when you start to use them, but try not to make the mistake of holding them too tightly. You will soon begin to judge the amount of pressure needed to prevent them from falling out of your hand which

Tea and wine

is all the pressure you need. After a remarkably short time you will suddenly notice that you eat with chopsticks almost automatically. When you want to practice using chopsticks, try picking up a marble that has been rubbed with oil or soap. If you manage to lift it, you have completely mastered the art of eating with chopsticks! Noodles, vegetables and slices of meat will present no problems, but peas and rice may prove more difficult to manage with chopsticks. Keep in mind, though, the fact that rice is shovelled straight from a bowl which is held close to the mouth. The chopsticks are held slightly apart and the rice is scooped up into your mouth rather than the grains being lifted between the chopsticks from a plate on the table. It is usually quite easy to eat Chinese food with chopsticks because all ingredients are cut in bite sized pieces, but even if you are served a whole fish or duck or other food that is not cut up, do not panic. It will be so tender that the morsels of meat or fish can be lifted off the bones very easily.

Tea and wine are the classical accompaniments to Chinese food. Tea is preferred to wine which, as a rule, is reserved for formal meals. Tea is drunk before, with and after the meal. The origin of tea is surrounded with many legends, and many tales are told of the ways its restorative qualities were discovered. It is certain that tea first appeared at least 2000 years ago and wine seems to be even older, though it is not possible to be quite sure in which age it was first drunk. The drinking of tea is not limited to a particular occasion or a specific hour of the day. The best way to welcome a guest is to present him with a cup of tea. Chinese tea is drunk for its subtle qualities of taste and fragrance. Sugar, milk or lemon are never added because any of these additions would ruin its bouquet. As with a wine, the quality and the characteristics of the tea are determined by a number of conditions such as the area and the soil in which it grows, the climate of the area and the way it is processed after it is harvested. Though there are many varieties of tea, there is an accepted classification which divides all of the teas into three groups according to the way in which they are processed. These groups are green tea, black tea and oolong.
For green tea, the top leaves are harvested and dried in the sun or in a drying house. Black tea is made from leaves which are not harvested until they have withered. The leaves are then

subjected to a process of rolling and fermenting before they are dried. With the oolong type, the fermentation or oxidizing process is stopped halfway and the leaves are only partly dried.

These processes result in three distinct types of tea. The green tea has leaves of a dull grayish green color and produces a pale lightly colored brew. Black tea produces a reddish brown brew that is much stronger in flavor. The oolong type produces a rich brew, golden amber in color. In China, teas are often scented with dried blossoms which are added to the leaves. Jasmine tea is a well known example.

For drinking tea, any small teacup will do. If you want to brew the tea directly in a teacup, however, you may find the Chinese teacup without a handle, but with a saucer and a lid, a valuable implement. The lid keeps the aroma inside and serves as a strainer for the tea leaves. When brewing black tea in a pot use about one teaspoon of tea, or slightly less, for every cup of water. For green tea use one teaspoon of tea for every four cups of water to start with, and regulate the amount of tea to your own taste the next time. When you are brewing in a cup, half a teaspoon or less of black tea will prove sufficient and even less for green teas. When brewing in a pot, it is best to add only small quantities of water at first, and let it steep, covered, for about forty-five seconds. Then add the rest of the water,

and steep an additional two and a half minutes.

Wine, apart from having an important role to play in the kitchen, is not normally drunk with a family meal but may appear at formal banquets for special occasions and as an accompaniment to savories. One could easily be misled by the word wine because no grapes are ever used in the preparation of Chinese wines. Instead they are distilled from rice, wheat and other grains. Wine is drunk from small china cups and is usually served hot. Apart from the wines distilled from grains, there are some made from fruits, such as plums. For cooking, not drinking, Chinese rice wine may be replaced by a dry sherry. Wines such as yellow Shao Shing rice wine is made in various grades, and the grade which is used for cooking purposes is not fit to drink with food. If you cannot find any rice wine to drink, you might like to try Japanese Sake which is more readily available and is a very satisfactory alternative.

Basic preparations

Rice cooking I

4 American servings
4 Chinese servings

   1 cup raw long grain white rice
1½ to 1¾ cups water

Put the rice in a large saucepan. Add enough cold water to cover the rice by 2 inches. Wash the rice by rubbing it gently between your fingers. Drain and cover rice with fresh water. Continue washing the rice until the water is clear. This washing process removes dust and excess starch from the rice. Put the rice into a large saucepan. Add the water and bring to boiling point over moderately high heat. Stir rice occasionally until most of the water has been absorbed and the rice is visible, bubbling and foaming. Cover the pan and reduce heat to simmering point. Continue cooking for 20 minutes until the rice is dry and fluffy.

Note: You may need to adjust the quantity of water and the length of the cooking time depending on the type of rice which you are using. Unfortunately, exact timing can only be judged after a few experiments.

Rice cooking II

4 American servings
4 Chinese servings

   1 cup raw long grain white rice
Water

Wash the rice as directed in the previous recipe. Place the rice in a large saucepan in an even layer. Add enough cold water to cover the rice by 1 inch. Bring to a boil over high heat. Stir once. Cover and simmer over low heat for 25 minutes until all the water has been absorbed. Do not raise the lid while the rice is simmering. Stir cooked rice gently to separate and fluff the grains. If the rice is not used immediately, leave it covered over the lowest possible heat. Do not turn off the heat and then turn it on again or the rice will become soft and pasty.

Rice steaming

4 American servings
4 Chinese servings

   1 cup raw long grain white rice
Water

Wash the rice as described in recipe for rice cooking I. Place in a pan with plenty of water. Bring to a boil over high heat and boil for 5 to 7 minutes, stirring occasionally. Drain in a sieve. Transfer rice to a steamer lined with a piece of cloth. Cover with the lid and steam for about 20 minutes. Little holes can be made in the rice with a chopstick to ensure better steaming.

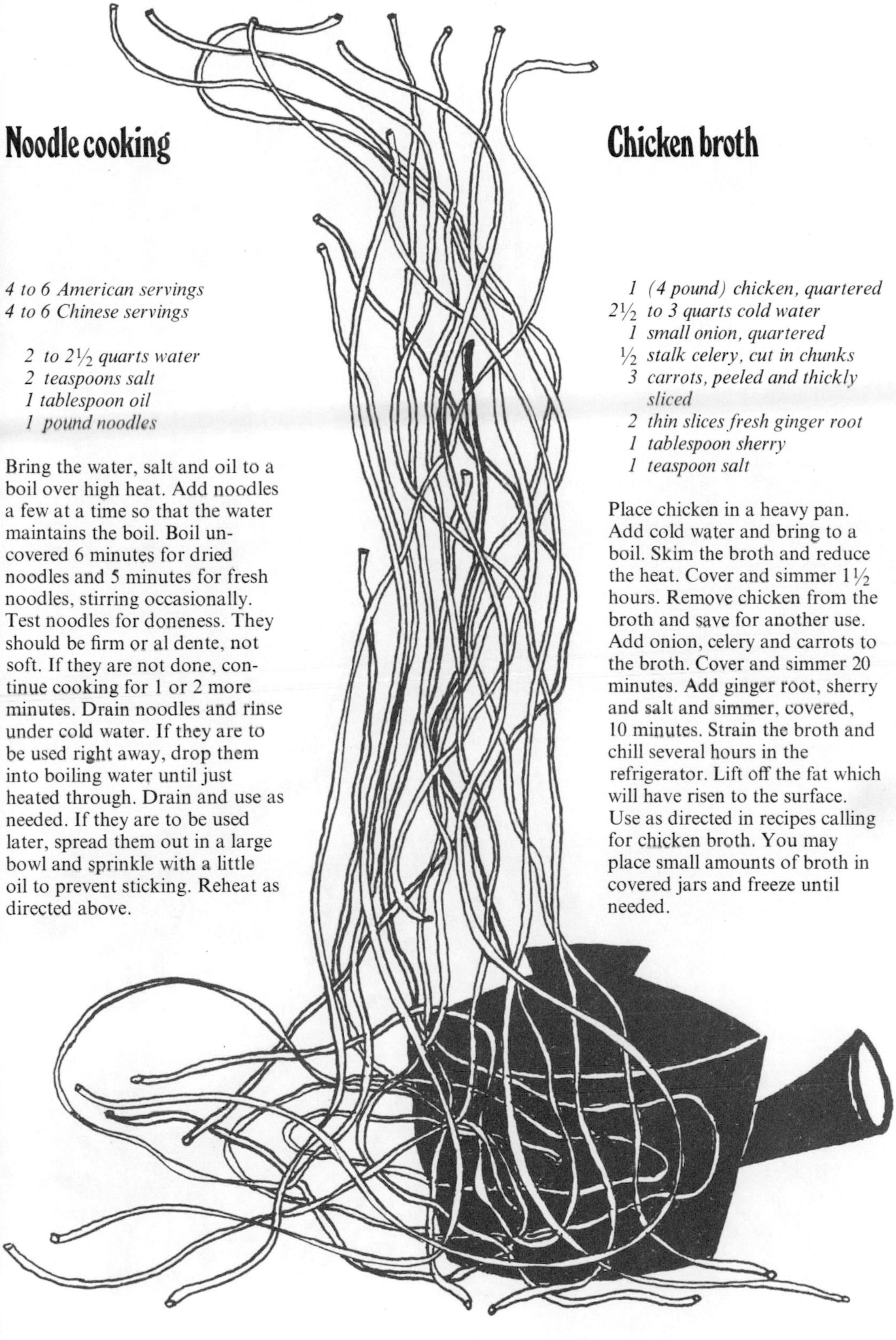

Noodle cooking

4 to 6 American servings
4 to 6 Chinese servings

2 to 2½ quarts water
2 teaspoons salt
1 tablespoon oil
1 pound noodles

Bring the water, salt and oil to a
boil over high heat. Add noodles
a few at a time so that the water
maintains the boil. Boil uncovered 6 minutes for dried
noodles and 5 minutes for fresh
noodles, stirring occasionally.
Test noodles for doneness. They
should be firm or al dente, not
soft. If they are not done, continue cooking for 1 or 2 more
minutes. Drain noodles and rinse
under cold water. If they are to
be used right away, drop them
into boiling water until just
heated through. Drain and use as
needed. If they are to be used
later, spread them out in a large
bowl and sprinkle with a little
oil to prevent sticking. Reheat as
directed above.

Chicken broth

1 (4 pound) chicken, quartered
2½ to 3 quarts cold water
1 small onion, quartered
½ stalk celery, cut in chunks
3 carrots, peeled and thickly
sliced
2 thin slices fresh ginger root
1 tablespoon sherry
1 teaspoon salt

Place chicken in a heavy pan.
Add cold water and bring to a
boil. Skim the broth and reduce
the heat. Cover and simmer 1½
hours. Remove chicken from the
broth and save for another use.
Add onion, celery and carrots to
the broth. Cover and simmer 20
minutes. Add ginger root, sherry
and salt and simmer, covered,
10 minutes. Strain the broth and
chill several hours in the
refrigerator. Lift off the fat which
will have risen to the surface.
Use as directed in recipes calling
for chicken broth. You may
place small amounts of broth in
covered jars and freeze until
needed.

Meat broth

2 pounds lean pork pieces with
bone
3 to 4 chicken wings, necks,
back pieces, etc.
2 quarts water
1 small onion, quartered
2 carrots, peeled and thickly
sliced
2 slices fresh ginger root
½ teaspoon salt
2 teaspoons soy sauce

Place pork and chicken pieces in
a heavy pan. Add water and
bring to a boil. Skim the broth,
boil 5 minutes and skim again.
Reduce heat, cover and simmer
20 minutes. Add onion, carrots
and ginger root and simmer,
covered, 30 minutes more. Add
salt and soy sauce and simmer
5 minutes. Strain the broth and
refrigerate several hours. Lift off
the fat which will have risen to
the surface. Use as directed in
recipes calling for meat broth.
Meat broth may be frozen as
indicated in the previous recipe.

Egg roll skins

14 skins

  2 *cups sifted all purpose flour*
½ *teaspoon salt*
  2 *eggs, lightly beaten*
1¾ *cups water*
  2 *tablespoons oil*

Sift the flour and salt into a bowl. Make a well in the center and add the eggs. Stir until well blended. Add the water gradually. Continue stirring with a wire whisk until the batter is smooth. Pour 1 tablespoon oil in a heavy 8 inch skillet. Heat until oil is hot. Tip out the excess oil, leaving a thin film of oil in the skillet. Pour about 2 tablespoons of batter into the oiled skillet. Tilt the pan in all directions to spread the batter evenly and thinly over the surface of the pan. Cook over low heat for 1½ minutes until firm but not brown. Cook on 1 side only. Stack the pancakes on a plate and cover with a damp cloth to prevent them from drying out. Brush the skillet with oil before cooking each pancake. Let pancakes cool completely before filling. Egg roll skins can also be made by the same method as wonton wrappers (see recipe on this page). Add only ¼ teaspoon salt and twice as much ice-cold water as called for in the wonton recipe. Cut the dough into 7 to 8 inch squares.

Wonton wrappers

40 to 50 wrappers

2 *cups all purpose flour*
1 *teaspoon salt*
1 *egg, lightly beaten*
3 to 4 *tablespoons water*
    Cornstarch for dusting

Sift the flour and salt together into a bowl. Make a well in the center and add the egg and 2 tablespoons water. Mix until well blended. Add the remaining water a little at a time, using only enough to make the dough hold together. Knead dough until smooth. Cover the bowl with a damp cloth and refrigerate 45 minutes. Dust a board lightly with cornstarch. Divide the dough into 2 pieces and roll out paper thin (not more than 1/16 inch). Cut dough into 3 inch squares. Cover wrappers with a damp cloth until you are ready to use them.

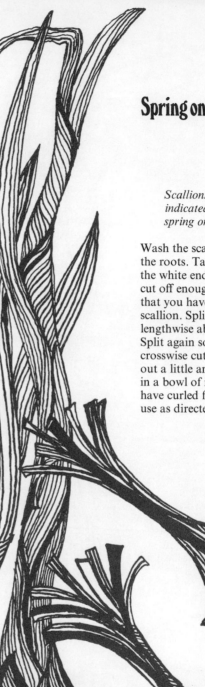

Spring onion brushes

Scallions (quantity as indicated in recipe requiring spring onion brushes)

Wash the scallions and remove the roots. Take a thin slice from the white end of the scallion and cut off enough of the green so that you have a 2 to 2½ inch scallion. Split the scallion in half lengthwise about ⅓ the way up. Split again so that you have a crosswise cut. Spread the cut end out a little and place scallions in a bowl of ice water until they have curled fringes. Drain and use as directed.

21

Shredded lettuce and radish garnish

Lettuce leaves as well as shredded lettuce can be used as a garnish or to make a bed for serving other ingredients. To prepare lettuce leaves, select several large, beautiful leaves. Wash and dry them and arrange attractively on a serving dish or plate. For the shredded lettuce, wash and drain several leaves. Place them one on top of another and cut uniform strips about ¼ inch wide. Place the shredded lettuce on a plate and use as a bed for the remaining ingredients.

Radishes can be used in several ways to form an attractive garnish. To make radish roses, cut off the green tops and a very small part of the bottom of the radish so that it can stand upright without tipping. With a very sharp knife, make a circular incision about 1/16 inch away from the skin. Then cut out small triangles with the base at the top and the tip pointing downward. Place the radishes in ice water and refrigerate for about 20 minutes so that they open like roses. Another method is to cut away small half circles or crescents to suggest leaves.

Radish fans can be made in the following way. Place the radish, preferably a perfectly oval one, lengthwise between 2 knitting needles or pieces of wire. Cut it crosswise in 1/16 inch thick slices. The needles will prevent you from cutting completely through the radish. Place the radishes in a small bowl. Sprinkle with a few teaspoons of salt and sugar

and toss to coat. Refrigerate for 5 to 10 minutes or until wilted. Rinse the radishes under cold running water and spread them into fans or flowers.

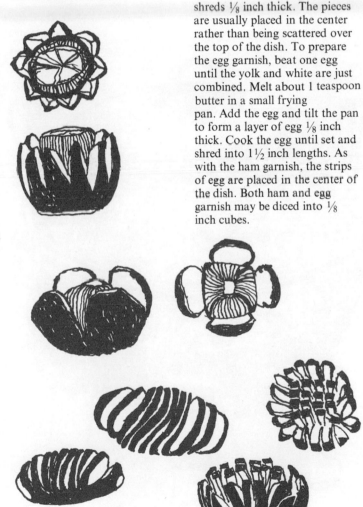

Ham and egg garnish

Both shredded ham and egg are frequently used to garnish soups and other dishes. To prepare the ham garnish, cut a thick slice of boiled or smoked ham into shreds ⅛ inch thick. The pieces are usually placed in the center rather than being scattered over the top of the dish. To prepare the egg garnish, beat one egg until the yolk and white are just combined. Melt about 1 teaspoon butter in a small frying pan. Add the egg and tilt the pan to form a layer of egg ⅛ inch thick. Cook the egg until set and shred into 1½ inch lengths. As with the ham garnish, the strips of egg are placed in the center of the dish. Both ham and egg garnish may be diced into ⅛ inch cubes.

Chicken velvet

1 whole boneless chicken breast
4 tablespoons water
½ teaspoon salt
1 teaspoon cornstarch
3 egg whites

Remove outer skin, tendons and other trimmings from chicken breast. Beat the meat with the flat side of a cleaver for about 1 minute. Remove as much inner fat, tendons and gristle as possible. Mince meat on a chopping board and remove any additional tendons and gristle. Continue mincing the meat until it becomes a smooth purée. Add drops of water (1 tablespoon total) as you are mincing to make the velvet smooth. Place the meat in a bowl with the salt and cornstarch and mix thoroughly. Add remaining 3 tablespoons water and 1 egg white. Place mixture in a blender and blend until smooth. Beat remaining egg whites until stiff and fold them into the velvet. Use as directed in sweet corn and chicken soup (recipe page 24) or poached chicken balls (recipe page 48).

Soups

There is an immense variety of soups in Chinese cooking, some are light and clear and others are thick and filling. They may be either bland and served to clear the palate, or spicy and pungent, served to form a contrast with other foods. They range from an inexpensive and simple bouillon with a few greens or some egg threads added, to very costly and time-consuming preparations, like shark's fin soup. Most soups have a short cooking time, though some thick and hearty soups, which have dried or salted ingredients added for extra flavor, require a longer time. Most green vegetables are only added in the last few minutes so they will retain their crispness and bright color. When tougher vegetables, like carrots, are used, they are parboiled first and then added with the more tender leafy vegetables. The basis of a soup can be water, but more frequently a light, though rich, bouillon will be used. Soy sauce, ginger juice and sesame oil are often added in small quantities for extra flavor. Though some soups are eaten to begin the meal, they are also served as a wonderful accompaniment to rice dishes. There are a number of sweet soups in Chinese cooking which are served only at formal dinners or banquets, and these are customarily eaten at the end of a meal.

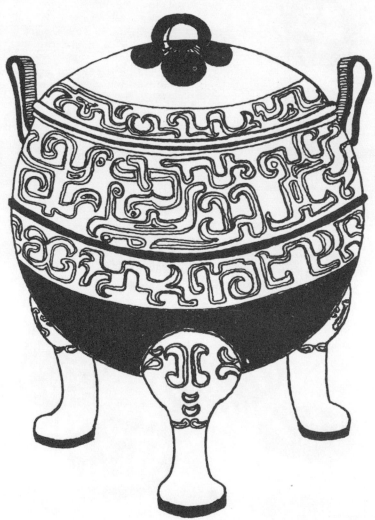

Pork and cucumber soup

4 American servings
4 Chinese servings

- ¾ teaspoon cornstarch
- ¼ teaspoon salt
  Pinch of white pepper
- 1 teaspoon sherry
- 2 ounces lean pork, cut across the grain into thin slices
- 3 cups meat broth (recipe page 19)
- ¼ cucumber, peeled, seeded and cut into strips
- 1½ teaspoons soy sauce

Mix cornstarch, salt, pepper and sherry in a bowl. Add pork strips and toss to coat. Bring broth to a boil and add pork. Reduce heat, cover and simmer 5 minutes. Add cucumber and simmer 3 more minutes. Stir in soy sauce and serve.

Peking hot sour soup

4 to 6 American servings
4 to 6 Chinese servings

  4 *dried Chinese mushrooms*
 ½ *cup lean pork*
 ⅓ *cup canned bamboo shoots*
  2 *bean curd cakes*
  1 *egg*
  1 *tablespoon cornstarch*
  4 *tablespoons water*
  4 *cups chicken broth*
  2 *tablespoons white vinegar*
  1 *tablespoon soy sauce*
 ¼ *teaspoon salt*
 ¼ *teaspoon freshly ground
     pepper*
 ½ *teaspoon sesame oil*
  1 *scallion, minced*

Soak dried mushrooms in hot
water for 20 minutes. Squeeze
dry and remove stems. Cut
mushroom caps into thin strips.
Cut pork across the grain in
¼ inch thick slices and then in ⅛
inch wide strips. Cut bean curd
and bamboo shoots into similar
sized strips. Break egg in a bowl
and beat lightly. Mix cornstarch
and water until well blended.
Bring the broth to the boil and
add pork and mushrooms. Bring
to the boil again, reduce heat
and simmer for about 8 to 10
minutes. Add the bamboo shoots
and bean curd and simmer
another 4 to 5 minutes. Mix
vinegar, soy sauce, salt and
pepper and stir into soup. Stir
in cornstarch mixture and cook
stirring constantly until
thickened. Stir in the beaten egg
and remove from heat when egg
threads are almost firm. Add
sesame oil and scallion and
serve immediately.

Watercress soup

4 American servings
4 Chinese servings

 ½ *bunch watercress*
  3 *cups chicken broth (recipe
     page 19)*
 ½ *teaspoon minced fresh
     ginger root*
 ½ *teaspoon soy sauce*
 ½ *teaspoon sherry*
 ¼ *cup slivered lean pork*
  1 *scallion, shredded*
 ¼ *teaspoon salt*

Wash watercress, discard tough
stems and cut in 1½ inch
lengths. In a saucepan, combine
broth, ginger root, soy sauce
and sherry and bring to a boil.
Add pork, reduce heat and
simmer for 10 minutes. Add
watercress, scallion and salt and
simmer for another 2 to 3
minutes. Serve immediately.

Pork and abalone soup

4 American servings
4 Chinese servings

  1 *(4 ounce) can abalone*
 ¾ *cup (4 ounces) lean pork*
  4 *cups chicken broth*
  2 *tablespoons sherry*
 ¼ *cup bamboo shoots*
  2 *tablespoons oil*
 ½ *teaspoon salt*
  2 *thin slices fresh ginger root*
 ⅛ *teaspoon freshly ground
     black pepper*
  4 *sprigs parsley*

Drain abalone and reserve the
liquid. Cut the abalone and the
pork into 1½ inch squares,
⅛ inch thick. Combine abalone
liquid, chicken broth and sherry.
Cut bamboo shoots into ⅛ inch
thick slices and cut slices into
match stick size strips 1½ inches
long. Heat chicken broth mixture
to boiling point. Heat the
oil in a wok or skillet. Add salt.
Add ginger root and stir fry for
2 minutes until lightly browned.
Discard ginger root. Add the
pork and stir fry for 2 minutes or
until meat turns white and loses
all its pink color. Do not let the
pork brown. Transfer the pork to
the saucepan containing boiling
chicken broth. Add abalone
and bamboo to the broth.
Season with pepper. Cook only
to heat through or abalone will
toughen. Serve in individual
bowls. Float a parsley sprig in
each bowl.

Crab asparagus soup

6 American servings
6 Chinese servings

  8 *ounces fresh crabmeat*
  1 *pound fresh, thin stemmed
     asparagus*
  1 *tablespoon sherry*
 ½ *tablespoon soy sauce*
  6 *cups chicken broth*
  1 *tablespoon oil*
  1 *scallion, minced*
  1 *tablespoon cornstarch*
  3 *tablespoons water*
1½ *teaspoons chili sauce or*
 ½ *teaspoon Chinese chili paste*
  1 *tablespoon finely chopped
     chives*

Flake the crabmeat and remove
hard membranes. Cut the top
third of asparagus flowers and
stems into pieces 1½ inches long.
Parboil asparagus in boiling
salted water for 3 minutes. Bring
sherry, soy sauce and chicken
broth to boiling point. Drain and
rinse asparagus under cold
running water. Heat the oil in a
wok or skillet. Add scallion and
stir fry for 30 seconds. Add
crabmeat and asparagus and stir
fry for 30 seconds. Add
crabmeat and asparagus to
chicken broth. Add chilli sauce.
Stir in cornstarch dissolved in
cold water. Stir 1 minute to
thicken broth slightly. Ladle into
bowls and garnish with chives.

24

Wonton soup

4 *American servings*
4 *Chinese servings*

For the wontons:
   8 *wonton wrappers (recipe*
       page 20)
   1 *dried Chinese mushroom*
   ⅓ *cup lean minced pork or beef*
   ¼ *cup minced shrimp*
   1 *water chestnut, minced*
   1 *whole scallion, minced*
   ½ *teaspoon soy sauce*
   1 *teaspoon sherry*
       Pinch of sugar
   ¼ *teaspoon salt*
   1 *egg, lightly beaten*

For the soup:
   3 *cups chicken broth (recipe*
       page 19)
   1 *scallion, white part only,*
       thinly sliced
   2 *tablespoons egg garnish*
       (recipe page 21)

Soak dried mushroom in warm
water 20 minutes. Squeeze dry.
Remove the stalk and mince the
cap. Combine mushroom, pork,
shrimp, water chestnut, scallion,
soy sauce, sherry, sugar and salt.
Let stand 30 minutes. Place
½ teaspoon of the filling barely
off center of each wrapper. Fold
wrapper in half and press the
edges together to seal them.
Again, fold the wrapper in half.
Pull the corners down into a
crescent shape, overlapping the
corners. Seal the overlap with a
little of the beaten egg. Bring
plenty of salted water to a
boil. Drop in the wontons one
by one and simmer 7 minutes.
(Make sure they do not stick to
the bottom of the pan.) Drain
the wontons. Bring the chicken

broth to a boil. Add wontons
and scallion. Top each serving
with a little of the egg garnish.

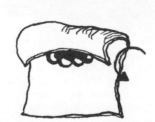

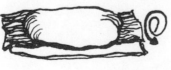

Egg drop soup

4 *American servings*
4 *Chinese servings*

   1 *egg*
   ½ *teaspoon water*
   3 *cups chicken or meat broth*
       (recipes page 19)
   ⅛ *teaspoon sugar*
   ¼ *teaspoon salt*
   ⅛ *teaspoon sesame oil*
   1 *small scallion, minced*
   2 *teaspoons finely chopped*
       chives

In a small bowl, beat the egg
with the water. Bring the broth
to a simmer and stir in the sugar,
salt and sesame oil. Continue to
stir and slip the egg into the
simmering broth. As you stir,
the egg will coagulate and form
thin threads. Stir in the scallion
and remove from the heat. Pour
soup into individual bowls.
Garnish with chives and serve.

Sweet corn and chicken soup

4 *American servings*
4 *Chinese servings*

   1 *(4 ounce) can creamed corn*
   3 *cups chicken broth*
   ¼ *teaspoon salt*
   1 *teaspoon cornstarch*
       dissolved in
   1 *tablespoon water*
   ½ *recipe chicken velvet*
       (recipe page 21)
   1 *tablespoon ham garnish*
       (recipe page 21)

Place corn in a blender and
blend until smooth. Bring the
broth to the simmering point.
Add the corn and salt and
simmer 3 minutes. Stir in
cornstarch mixture to thicken
slightly. Add chicken velvet and
simmer 1 minute, stirring
constantly. Pour into individual
soup bowls, top with ham
garnish and serve.

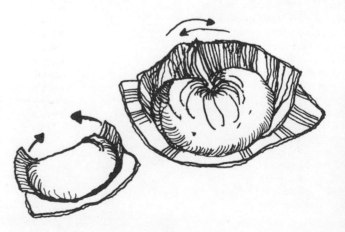

Three famous Chinese soups: Sweet corn and chicken soup, wonton soup (recipe page 24, 1st and 4th column), pork and abalone soup, (recipe page 23, 3rd column).

Appetizers

The Chinese are fond of appetizers. They like to start off a meal with them and accordingly have developed a wonderful range of mouth-watering tidbits to be sampled before the real dinner starts. They are also lunch time favorites. Apart from the dishes listed in this book, there are thousands of others, and in China all sorts of dried nuts and seeds are also served at formal dinners. Great attention is paid to the presentation of the appetizers. This category includes a great many steamed and deep fried foods as well as cold dishes and salads. Many of the appetizers are listed under other headings such as the salads, which are to be found among the vegetable dishes; the shrimp balls, which are listed under seafood, and poultry dishes such as drunken chicken. They can be served either as appetizer or luncheon dishes. On the other hand some of them can be served as snacks in between other more elaborate dishes.

Egg rolls

14 rolls

1 recipe egg roll skins (see page 20)
½ pound lean pork
¼ pound shrimp
1½ to 2 cups bean sprouts
3 tablespoons lard or oil
8 whole scallions, finely chopped
½ cup bamboo, shredded
8 water chestnuts, cut into ⅛ inch slices
3 thin slices ginger root, minced
½ teaspoon salt
½ tablespoon soy sauce
½ tablespoon sherry
1 egg, lightly beaten
Oil for deep frying

Prepare the egg roll skins according to the recipe. Cut the pork across the grain in ¼ inch thick slices and then into strips. Mince the strips finely. Shell the shrimp. Remove the vein and chop shrimp into very small pieces. Rinse the bean sprouts under cold running water. Heat 2 tablespoons of the lard or oil in a wok or a skillet. Add the pork and stir fry for 1½ to 2 minutes until it turns white and loses any trace of pink. Add shrimp and stir fry for 45 seconds. Remove from the pan and add remaining tablespoon of lard or oil. Heat until hot. Add scallions, bamboo, water chestnuts and ginger root. Stir fry for 1½ minutes. Add bean sprouts and stir fry for 45 seconds. Return pork and shrimp to the pan. Add salt, soy sauce and sherry and heat through. Remove from the heat. Place in a colander to drain and cool completely. Divide the mixture into 16 parts.

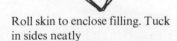

Place one part slightly off the center of each skin

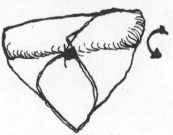

Roll skin to enclose filling. Tuck in sides neatly

Brush opposite side with beaten egg

Continue rolling egg rolls. Place them on a plate with sealed edge down. Fry the egg rolls in deep fat for 3 to 4 minutes. Turn the rolls once to brown evenly on all sides. Drain and serve hot

Siu mai pork dumplings

20 dumplings

Filling:
¾ cup lean ground pork
¼ cup minced fat pork
1 tablespoon minced bamboo shoots
1½ tablespoons minced water chestnuts
1½ tablespoons chopped mushrooms
1 tablespoon sherry
1 teaspoon soy sauce
⅛ teaspoon salt
⅛ teaspoon sugar
Pinch of white pepper
1 egg white, lightly beaten

½ recipe wonton wrapper dough (recipe page 20)

Mix all of the ingredients for the filling in a bowl until well combined. Roll out the dough as described on page 20 and cut it into 3 inch rounds. Place a spoonful of the filling on each round. Gather the dough up around the filling, leaving the dough slightly open and the edges flared. Drop each dumpling on the board a few times to flatten the bottom. Place dumplings in a steamer and steam 20 to 25 minutes.

Shrimp toast II

6 American servings
8 Chinese servings

½ pound medium sized shrimp
1 thin slice fresh ginger root
2 eggs
1½ tablespoons minced onion
1 teaspoon salt
⅛ teaspoon freshly ground pepper
1 teaspoon sherry
1 teaspoon cornstarch
4 slices day old bread
Oil for deep frying
1 tablespoon minced lean cooked ham

Shell the shrimp and take out the black vein. Mince the shrimp together with the ginger. Beat the eggs. In a bowl mix shrimp, ginger, onion, salt, pepper, sherry, cornstarch and slightly more than half of the beaten egg. Mix until well blended. Cut the crusts off the bread and spread with the shrimp mixture. Cut each slice into 4 triangles and brush lightly with the remaining egg. Heat the oil for deep frying until hot. Immerse shrimp toasts carefully, a few at a time, into the hot oil, shrimp side down. Deep fry for about 1½ minutes. Turn the pieces over and deep fry for 20 more seconds. Remove from pan and drain on paper towels. Sprinkle with minced ham and serve immediately.

Shrimp toast I

6 American servings
8 Chinese servings

½ pound shrimp
4 water chestnuts, minced
1 very thin slice ginger root, minced
1 egg, lightly beaten
¼ teaspoon sugar
½ teaspoon salt
⅛ teaspoon freshly ground pepper
2 teaspoons sherry
2 teaspoons cornstarch
4 slices firm textured day old bread
Oil for deep frying

Shell the shrimp and remove the black vein. Mince the shrimp finely. Place the shrimp in a bowl and add water chestnuts, ginger root, egg, sugar, salt, pepper, sherry and cornstarch. Mix until all the ingredients are well combined. Remove the crusts from the bread. Cut each slice of bread into 4 squares or rectangles. Divide the shrimp mixture into 16 equal portions. Spread each piece of bread with the shrimp mixture. Heat the oil. Add shrimp toasts and deep fry a few at a time until bread is lightly browned; about 1½ minutes. Remove toasts and drain on paper towels. Increase the heat under the oil and deep fry the toasts a second time for 30 seconds. Bread will be crisp and well browned. Drain on paper towels. Serve immediately.

Har kau shrimp dumplings

2 to 3 American servings
2 to 3 Chinese servings

2 to 3 giant shrimp, shelled and deveined
1 ounce cooked ham fat
½ teaspoon salt
2 teaspoons sherry
3 ounces Chinese wheat starch

Coarsely dice the shrimp and ham fat together. Add salt and sherry and mix until well blended. Combine the wheat starch with enough water to make a firm paste. Place the paste in a sheet on a plate and steam for about 5 minutes. Remove it from the pan and, as soon as it can be handled, form it into a roll. Divide the roll into 6 to 8 uniformly sized rounds and press or roll out one round to a diameter of 2 to 3 inches. Keep the other rounds hot and moist under a hot, damp towel. Divide the stuffing in as many portions as there are rounds. Place one portion of the filling in the center of the round of dough; fold over to form a half moon shape; press down on the edges and pinch the dumpling into the shape of a Dutch bonnet. Prepare the remaining dumplings in the same manner as quickly as possible. Steam for 15 to 20 minutes and serve hot.
Note: The dough will be quite sticky and must be handled while still hot and moist. Otherwise the edges will not hold together during steaming.

Barbecued spareribs

4 American servings
6 Chinese servings

2 pounds spareribs

Barbecue sauce:
2 cloves garlic, crushed and minced
3 tablespoons soy sauce
1 tablespoon sherry
3 tablespoons hoisin sauce
1 tablespoon sugar
1 tablespoon honey
1 tablespoon chicken broth
1 tablespoon oil
6 to 8 onion brushes (see page 20)

Choose short boned spare ribs if possible. Remove fat from ribs and trim ribs neatly. Leave the sheet of ribs in 1 or 2 pieces but cut halfway between each rib. Combine all the remaining ingredients except the onion brushes. Pour sauce ingredients over the ribs and allow the ribs to marinate for 3 hours. Turn the ribs every hour. Place ribs on a foil covered rack and roast for 45 minutes in a 400 degree oven. Garnish with onion brushes and serve immediately.

Juicy barbequed spareribs and crisp deep fried wontons are a wonderful way to start a meal, (recipe page 27, 4th column).

Buns from the North (right) and Siu Mai dumplings (recipe page 26, 4th column) from the South in their bamboo steaming baskets. Red dots are usually

made on buns with a sweet stuffing to tell them apart from the ones that have juicy meat inside.

Steamed buns

24 buns

 1 package dry yeast
 1 tablespoon sugar
1¼ cups lukewarm water
3½ to 4 cups flour
 2 tablespoons oil
 4 scallions, minced
 1 clove garlic, crushed
 3 cups minced roast pork
      (recipe page 33)
 2 teaspoons sugar
 2 tablespoons soy sauce
 1 tablespoon sherry
1½ tablespoons cornstarch
      dissolved in
 3 tablespoons chicken broth
 2 teaspoons red food coloring

Sprinkle yeast and sugar over ¼ cup lukewarm water and stir to dissolve. Let stand 10 minutes. Add remaining 1 cup lukewarm water and mix well. Add the flour ½ cup at a time until approximately 3 cups have been added. Turn the dough out onto a floured board and knead the dough, incorporating as much of the additional flour as is necessary to keep it from sticking to the board and your hands. Continue to knead until the dough is smooth and satiny, about 7 minutes. Place the dough in an oiled bowl, cover with a towel and let rise until doubled in bulk (1 to 2 hours depending on the warmth of your kitchen). Meanwhile prepare the filling. Heat the oil in a wok. Stir fry the scallion and garlic for 1 minute. Add the pork and stir fry until heated through. Add the sugar, soy sauce and sherry and stir to blend. Add the dissolved

cornstarch and stir until thickened. Set the mixture aside to cool. Punch the dough down and knead on the floured board 3 minutes. Shape into a log about 2 inches in diameter. Cut the dough into 24 equal pieces. Roll each piece into a circle about 3 to 3½ inches in diameter. Divide the filling into 24 portions and place 1 portion in the center of each round of dough. Pull the sides of the dough up around the filling and pinch the edges together. With the palms of your hands, gently shape the buns into neat, round balls. Place on pieces of waxed paper, cover with a cloth and let rise 20 minutes. Place the buns in a steamer on their pieces of waxed paper and steam 20 minutes. or until glossy and smooth. Dip a chopstick in the red food coloring and make a dot on top of each bun. These buns may be made ahead and reheated by steaming again for a few minutes.

A little statue of Confucius seems to nod approvingly at the sight of this splendidly arranged platter of various neatly sliced cold meats. To him this is convincing proof that nowadays Chinese cooks still bear in mind the words he spoke centuries ago: Never serve food that is not properly cut.

Peacock platter

This dish received its name from the fact that various cold, thinly sliced meats are arranged on a platter to resemble the beautiful span of a peacock tail. No precise recipe can be given. It can be as extravagant or simple as time, money and ingenuity allow. Cooked ham, white cooked chicken, roast meats, abalone, braised duck and red simmered meats can be cut into equal sized, very thin slices. The slices can then be decorated as seen in the photograph. It is easiest to slice the meats with a commercial meat slicer, but, assuming that one is not available, be sure the meat is very cold or even partially frozen and your knife extremely sharp before you slice the meats. Asparagus, sliced hard boiled eggs, radishes, cucumber slices, carrot flowers, pineapple wedges, Chinese preserved eggs and many other things can be used for decoration. For instance, the slices of hard boiled egg topped with red and green fruit in the photograph represent the eye on the peacock feather. On top of the crisp roast belly of pork in the center and surrounding it are beautiful birds and flowers cut from carrots. Hoisin sauce and plum sauce can be served as dips on the side.

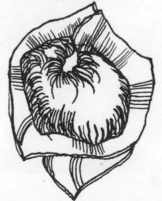

Deep fried wontons

6 to 8 American servings
6 to 8 Chinese servings

  20 to 24 wonton wrappers
      (recipe page 20)
   1 double recipe wonton filling
      as for soup wontons
      (recipe page 24)
   1 recipe sweet sour sauce I
      (recipe page 81)
   1 egg, lightly beaten
      Oil for deep frying

Prepare wonton wrappers, filling and sweet sour sauce as described in the indicated recipes. Shape the wontons as described in the recipe for wonton soup or follow these instructions. Divide the filling in 20 to 24 equal portions. Place 1 wrapper in front of you with a corner pointing toward you. Put a portion of the filling just a little off center towards you on the wrapper. Brush the edges of the wrapper very lightly with beaten egg. Fold over so the corner that pointed toward you just "misses" the opposite corner by ¼ to ½ inch. Press down on the wrapper around the filling to expel the air and seal the wonton. Brush a little of the beaten egg on the top of the right hand corner and the underside of the left hand corner. Pull both corners toward each other carefully and press them together. Heat the oil for deep frying until quite hot. Add the wontons a few at a time. Reduce the heat a little and deep fry until golden brown. Turn them over once during the frying. Remove with a skimmer or slotted spoon, drain on paper towels and serve hot with the sweet sour sauce on the side. Wontons may first be boiled, drained, dried thoroughly and then deep fried.

Stuffed mushrooms

4 American servings
4 Chinese servings

   8 large whole, undamaged
      Chinese dried mushrooms
  ¾ cup (4 ounces) lean pork,
      minced
   1 whole scallion, finely chopped
  ¼ teaspoon minced fresh ginger
      root
   1 tablespoon bamboo shoots
      or water chestnuts, minced
  ½ tablespoon soy sauce
  ½ tablespoon sherry
  ½ teaspoon oil
  ½ tablespoon finely chopped
      parsley

Soak the dried mushrooms in hot water for 30 minutes. Squeeze mushrooms to remove excess water. Cut off mushroom stems. In a bowl, combine pork, scallion, ginger root, bamboo shoots or water chestnuts, soy sauce, sherry and oil. Mix until well blended. Place mushrooms on a flat plate stem side up. Fill mushroom caps with stuffing. Place plate in a steamer with a lid or cover with foil. Steam over simmering water for 30 minutes. Sprinkle with parsley. Serve hot as an appetizer.

Deep fried paper wrapped shrimp

4 American servings
4 Chinese servings

   4 large shrimp
  ¼ teaspoon salt
  ¼ teaspoon white pepper
   1 clove garlic, crushed
   2 teaspoons sherry
   4 pieces of waxed paper,
      8 inches square
   1 tablespoon oil
   4 thin strips of red sweet
      pepper
   1 scallion, white part only,
      quartered lengthwise
   4 thin slices fresh ginger root
      Oil for deep frying
      Shredded lettuce (recipe
      page 21)
   4 tomato wedges

Shell the shrimp and take out the black vein. Mix the shrimp with salt, pepper, garlic and sherry and leave for at least 15 minutes. Toss occasionally. Drain. Rub one side of the pieces of waxed paper with the oil. Place 1 shrimp on top of each piece of paper diagonally just off center. Line with 1 pepper strip, 1 piece of scallion and 1 slice ginger. Fold the paper as illustrated in the picture. Heat oil for deep frying until hot, but not smoking (about 350 to 360°), and deep fry the shrimp for about 5 minutes. Remove with a slotted spoon and drain. Place the packages, unopened, on shredded lettuce and garnish each with a tomato wedge. Excellent to start off a meal, especially when served with salt and pepper mix (recipe page 83) and plum sauce (recipe page 83).

Pork

Stir fried pork, nuts and vegetables

3 American servings
6 Chinese servings

   3 dried Chinese mushrooms
½ pound lean pork (tenderloin, butt or shoulder)
½ cup bamboo, sliced
   6 water chestnuts
   2 scallions
   4 fresh mushrooms
   4 tablespoons oil
½ teaspoon salt
   1 clove garlic, crushed
   2 thin slices fresh ginger root
½ cup bean sprouts
½ teaspoon salt
   1 tablespoon sherry
½ cup chicken or meat broth
   1 tablespoon soy sauce
   1 tablespoon cornstarch dissolved in
   3 tablespoons water

Soak the dried mushrooms in hot water for about 30 minutes. Squeeze dry, remove stalks and cut caps in ¼ to ½ inch wide strips. Cut the pork across the grain into ⅛ inch thick slices. Cut the bamboo in ⅛ to ¼ inch slices and the water chestnuts cut in ¼ inch thick slices. Cut the scallions in 1 inch long pieces diagonally. Cut mushrooms in ¼ inch thick slices. Heat 2 tablespoons oil in a wok or other pan. Add the salt and stir fry for 30 seconds. Add the garlic and ginger and stir fry for about 45 seconds or until lightly browned. Remove garlic from pan. Add bamboo, water chestnuts, mushrooms and Chinese mushrooms and stir fry for 1 minute. Add bean sprouts and stir for another 30 to 45 seconds. Remove from the pan.

Add remaining oil and heat. Add salt and scallions and stir fry for 30 seconds. Add the pork and stir fry for about 2½ minutes. Stir in sherry and stir fry to blend. Return vegetables to the pan, add broth and soy sauce and bring quickly to a boil. Reduce heat, cover and simmer for about 2 minutes or until tender. Stir in the cornstarch mixture to thicken and serve immediately.

Stir fried pork and eggplant

4 American servings
8 Chinese servings

   1 large eggplant
   3 tablespoons salt
   1 tablespoon sherry
½ teaspoon salt
   2 teaspoons cornstarch
½ pound lean pork, cut diagonally across the grain into ⅛ inch slices
   3 tablespoons oil
¼ cup chicken broth
   2 tablespoons soy sauce
¼ teaspoon sugar
   2 cloves garlic, crushed
   1 thin slice fresh ginger root, minced
   4 scallions, cut diagonally into 1 inch pieces
   3 firm ripe tomatoes, peeled, seeded and cut into ½ inch slices

Remove the leaves from the eggplant and cut a ½ inch slice off both ends. Quarter the eggplant lengthwise, then cut into ½ inch slices. Sprinkle both sides of the pieces with salt and let stand 20 minutes to release the bitter juices. Rinse under cold running water and dry on paper towels. Combine the sherry, ½ teaspoon salt and cornstarch. Toss the pork strips in this mixture to coat them evenly. Heat half of the oil in a wok over high heat. Add the eggplant and stir fry 2 minutes. Add the broth, soy sauce and sugar. Reduce the heat a little, cover and cook 10 minutes. Remove eggplant and liquid from the pan. Wipe the wok dry with paper towels. Add remaining oil to the wok and

heat until very hot. Add garlic and ginger root and stir fry 1 minute. Discard garlic. Add pork and stir fry 1 minute. Add scallions and stir fry 2 minutes. Add tomatoes and stir fry ½ minute. Finally, return eggplant with its cooking liquid to the wok and stir about 1 minute. Transfer to a serving dish and serve immediately.

*Tender, pink pork is stir fried
with nuts and vegetables and
subtly flavored with a drop of
sesame oil.*

Stir fried pork, nuts and vegetables

2 American servings
4 Chinese servings

½ *pound lean pork (butt or
  shoulder)*
3 *to 4 stalks celery*
1 *small onion*
6 *to 8 carrots*
½ *red pepper*
1 *tablespoon soy sauce*
¼ *teaspoon sugar*
2 *teaspoons cornstarch*
3 *tablespoons oil*
¼ *teaspoon salt*
1 *clove garlic, crushed*
2 *thin slices fresh ginger root,
  minced*
¼ *cup roasted almonds or
  cashew nuts*
¼ *to ½ cup chicken broth*
1 *tablespoon soy sauce*
1 *tablespoon sherry*
1 *teaspoon sesame oil*
1 *tablespoon cornstarch*
3 *tablespoons water*

Cut pork in ⅛ to ¼ inch thick
slices across the grain. Trim
celery and cut in 1½ inch pieces
diagonally. Cut onion in half
lengthwise and then cut in 1 inch
pieces. Cut carrots in a rolling
cut diagonally into 1¼ inch long
pieces. Remove membrane and
seeds from red pepper and cut
into 2 inch long and ½ inch wide
strips. Mix soy sauce, sugar and
cornstarch. Add pork and toss to
coat. Bring plenty of salted water
to the boil, add the carrots and
parboil for about 4 minutes.
Rinse under cold running water
until completely cooled and
drain. Heat half of the oil in a
wok or other pan. Add salt and
stir fry for 30 seconds. Add pork
and stir fry for about 2½
minutes or until it has lost any
trace of pink. Remove from pan.
Add remaining oil and heat
until very hot. Add garlic and
ginger root and stir fry until
lightly browned. Discard garlic.
Add vegetables and almonds or
cashew nuts and stir fry for
about 1 minute. Add broth, soy
sauce, sherry and sesame oil and
bring quickly to the boil. Reduce
heat, cover and cook for about
2 to 2½ minutes. Return pork
and heat through. Dissolve
cornstarch in water and stir in to
thicken. Serve immediately.

*Egg plant and tomatoes are a
comparatively new addition to the
broad scale of flavors in Chinese
cooking. But a sensible one, as is
proved by this stir fried pork dish,
(recipe page 31, 3rd column).*

Pork is excellent when roasted. Roast pork figures as an important ingredient in a great variety of other dishes. Crisp roast belly of pork is accompanied by bean curd here.

Roast pork

4 American servings
8 Chinese servings

  2 *pounds boneless pork*
     tenderloin
  1 *clove garlic, crushed*
  3 *tablespoons soy sauce*
  1 *tablespoon sherry*
  1 *tablespoon hoisin sauce*
     Freshly ground black pepper
  2 *teaspoons sugar*
¼ *teaspoon ground cinnamon*
¼ *teaspoon ground anise*
  2 *tablespoons oil*
  2 *tablespoons honey*

Cut pork along the grain into pieces 6 inches long, 2 inches wide and 1 inch thick. Mix the remaining ingredients except the oil and honey in a shallow dish. Add the pork and coat it on all sides with the mixture. Let stand 2 to 3 hours, turning the pork slices once during the period. Drain and reserve the marinade. Transfer the pork to a rack with a drip pan underneath. Place a shallow pan of hot water on the bottom of a preheated 425° oven. Roast the pork in the oven 15 minutes. Combine 2 tablespoons reserved marinade with the oil. Brush the pork with this mixture. Turn the pork and brush the other side. Reduce heat to 350° and roast another 10 minutes. Brush the pork with honey. Turn the slices and brush the other side. Continue to roast 10 minutes. Remove from the oven and slice pork across the grain into ¼ inch thick slices. Serve hot or cold or use as directed in other recipes.

The meats used in Chinese cookery are pork, beef and lamb. Veal is almost never used, and lamb is rarely served except in the North. In the course of time the Chinese have developed numerous ways of preparing pork. It can be steamed, braised, red simmered, clear simmered stir fried, barbequed, roasted and deep fried, and it combines well with a vast number of other ingredients. Butt, shoulder and loin are good choices for almost any of these ways of preparing pork. Other parts of the pig including the feet, kidneys, pork belly, etc. are also used extensively in Chinese cooking. The color of the meat should be a bright pink.

Beef has historically always been scarce because cattle themselves are not raised extensively, and the small number of cattle that are found, are used to work on the fields. Beef is also prepared in many ways in Chinese cooking. Top round steak, flank steak, sirloin steak and tenderloin are the cuts most generally used. Flank steak is preferred because of its easily recognizable muscular structure. The color of the beef should be a beautiful red, and all the fat is trimmed away before it is cooked or served. Pork is done when all its pink color has gone and beef is done when there is no longer any trace of red and the meat is slightly browned. These color changes are important to watch for, especially in stir fried dishes.

Crisp roast belly of pork and bean curd

6 American servings
10 Chinese servings

 1 recipe roast belly of pork
   (see previous recipe)
 2 cakes bean curd
 2 to 3 tablespoons soy sauce
½ cup chicken broth
½ teaspoon salt
¼ teaspoon sugar
 1 tablespoon cornstarch
 2 tablespoons water
1½ tablespoons oil
   Few sprigs parsley

Prepare roast belly of pork as directed in previous recipe. Cut the pork into 1 to 1½ inch cubes. Cut bean curd cakes in 1½ inch long and ½ inch thick slices. Combine soy sauce, broth, salt and sugar in a saucepan and heat until salt and sugar are dissolved. Dissolve cornstarch in water. Heat the oil in a wok or other pan, add bean curd and stir fry for about 1 to 1½ minutes. Add soy sauce mixture, bring to the boil and stir in cornstarch to thicken. Stir in the pork. Decorate with parsley and serve.

Note: The bean curd in this recipe may be deep fried for 1½ minutes and added with the soy sauce mixture. If this method is used, just allow the bean curd to heat through again but do not stir fry.

Crisp roast belly of pork

6 American servings
8 Chinese servings

 2 pounds fresh belly of pork
   (fresh bacon)
 1 teaspoon salt
 1 tablespoon sugar or brown
   sugar
 3 tablespoons soy sauce
 1 tablespoon hoisin sauce
 1 thin slice fresh ginger root,
   minced
 1 small bunch watercress
 6 to 8 onion brushes (recipe
   page 20)

Prick the skin side of the pork belly with the point of a sharp knife and rub salt into the skin. Mix sugar, soy sauce, hoisin sauce and ginger and rub into the meat side. Place the meat, skin side up, on a rack under a preheated broiler and broil for 15 to 20 minutes or until skin is crisp and brown. Fill a pan with boiling water and place on the bottom of the oven. Place the broiler pan in the middle of the oven and roast the pork in a medium hot oven (350 to 375°) for about 1 hour or until done. Let cool to room temperature. Cut the pork into 1 inch cubes in such a way that every piece of meat has a piece of the skin. Place on a serving dish, surround with watercress and onion brushes and serve.

Braised pork

4 American servings
8 Chinese servings

2 pounds boneless fat pork
  (fresh ham or shoulder),
  in 1 piece
2 tablespoons oil
2 slices fresh ginger root,
  minced
1 clove garlic, crushed
2 scallions, cut diagonally
  into 1 inch pieces
6 tablespoons soy sauce
3 tablespoons sherry
3 cups boiling water
1½ tablespoons brown sugar

Heat oil in a heavy casserole.
Brown pork on all sides. Add
ginger root, garlic, and scallions
and cook 1 minute. Add soy
sauce, 2 tablespoons sherry and
water and bring to a simmer.
Reduce heat, cover the pan and
simmer 45 minutes, turning the
meat every 10 minutes. Add
the remaining sherry and the
brown sugar and cook 45
minutes to 1 hour, turning the
meat every 20 minutes. Slice
and serve moistened with a little
of the cooking liquid.

Red simmered pork

6 American servings
10 Chinese servings

½ pound dried Chinese squid,
  cleaned (optional)
¼ cup Chinese lily buds
  (optional)
3 pounds pork, preferably butt
2½ to 3 cups water
1 clove garlic, minced
3 slices fresh ginger root,
  minced
6 tablespoons soy sauce
1 tablespoon sherry
1 teaspoon salt
3 teaspoons brown sugar

If both squid and lily buds are
available, they give this dish a
very authentic character. On the
other hand, the pork will taste
excellent on its own. Soak squid
in warm water. Cut the body in
half lengthwise. Score the inside
with a sharp knife in a small
diamond pattern. Soak the lily
buds in warm water for about
1 hour. Rinse under cold water
and drain. Remove tough parts.
Cut pork into 1 to 1½ inch
cubes. Place in a heavy pan or
casserole, add the water and
bring to a boil over high heat.
Add garlic, ginger root, soy
sauce, sherry and salt. Bring to
a boil again. Reduce the heat,
cover and simmer for about ½
hour. Add the squid, cover and
simmer 40 minutes more. Add
lily buds and sugar. Cover and
simmer for another 30 to 40
minutes.

Tung po pork

4 American servings
8 Chinese servings

2 pounds pork loin with skin
2 tablespoons salt
4 cups water
2 scallions, cut into 1 inch
  pieces
4 tablespoons soy sauce
2 tablespoons sherry
1 thin slice fresh ginger root,
  minced
1 tablespoon sugar
1 cup shredded Chinese
  cabbage
1 tablespoon cornstarch
  dissolved in
3 tablespoons water

Cut pork in 3 inch squares and
rub with salt. Let stand 1 hour.
Rinse pork under cold running
water, place in a heavy pan with
the 4 cups water and bring to a
boil. Remove the pork with a
slotted spoon and rinse under
cold running water. Skim the
scum from the water and return
the pork to the pan. Cover and
simmer ½ hour. Add scallions,
soy sauce, sherry and ginger
root. Simmer, covered, 1½ hours
Remove the pork from the broth
and place, skin side down, in a
shallow heatproof dish. Sprinkle
with sugar, place in a steamer
and steam 45 minutes.
Meanwhile add the cabbage to
the broth and simmer 20
minutes. With a slotted spoon,
transfer cabbage to a serving
plate. Top with the pork, skin
side up. Add the dissolved
cornstarch to the simmering
broth and stir until thickened
slightly. Pour a few spoonfuls of
the sauce over the pork and serve.

Deep fried pork balls

4 to 6 American servings
4 to 6 Chinese servings

1½ pounds pork (loin, butt or
  shoulder) with some fat,
  minced
1 slice fresh ginger root,
  minced
3 water chestnuts, minced
½ medium onion, minced
1 teaspoon sugar
1 tablespoon soy sauce
2 teaspoons sherry
2½ tablespoons cornstarch
1 egg
  Oil for deep frying
  Shredded lettuce (see page
  21)

Combine the minced pork,
ginger, water chestnuts and
onion. Place these ingredients in
a bowl and mix thoroughly
with sugar, soy sauce, sherry,
cornstarch and egg. Form the
mixture into 10 to 15 balls and
place balls on a plate. Chill the
balls until ready to fry. Heat the
oil for deep frying. Add a few
balls at a time. Fry for about
3 minutes. Remove and drain on
paper towels. Continue frying
remaining pork balls a few at a
time. Reheat the oil until it is
very hot. Deep fry all the balls
together a second time for about
2 minutes until lightly browned
and crisp. Drain and serve on a
bed of shredded lettuce. Serve
plain or with a sweet sour
sauce (see pages 81 and 82) or
use in other recipes.

Sweet sour pork

4 American servings
8 Chinese servings

1 recipe sweet sour sauce I
   (recipe page 81)
1 pound lean pork
¼ teaspoon salt
¼ teaspoon sugar
1 tablespoon soy sauce
2 tablespoons sherry
⅛ teaspoon freshly ground
   black pepper
1 small onion
1 green pepper
2 slices canned pineapple
2 carrots, cut diagonally into
   1 inch pieces
1 egg
2 tablespoons flour

½ teaspoon salt
1 tablespoon water
2 tablespoons oil
2 thin slices fresh ginger root,
   minced
1 clove garlic, crushed
   Oil for deep frying

Combine ingredients for sweet sour sauce in an enamelled saucepan. Mix cornstarch and water for the sauce but do not add it yet. Cut the pork in pieces 1 to 1½ inches square and ¾ inch thick. Mix salt, sugar, soy sauce, sherry and pepper. Add pork, toss to coat and marinate for about 20 minutes, turning meat twice.

Cut the onion in half lengthwise and then cut into 1 to 1½ inch long and ¾ inch wide pieces. Remove membrane and seeds from pepper, cut in 1 inch wide strips and then in 1 to 1½ inch diamond shapes diagonally. Cut the pineapple rings into 1 inch pieces. Bring plenty of salted water to a boil, add the carrots and parboil for 3 to 4 minutes. Rinse under cold running water and drain. Combine egg, flour, salt and water to make a batter. Heat 2 tablespoons of oil in a wok or other pan. Add ginger and garlic and stir fry for 30 seconds. Discard garlic. Add vegetables and stir fry for about

2½ minutes. Meanwhile, heat the sweet sour sauce in a saucepan. Add sauce to the vegetables and stir in cornstarch mixture to thicken. Remove from heat and keep warm. Heat the oil for deep frying. Coat pork pieces lightly with the batter. Drop into the hot oil one by one and deep fry for about 3½ minutes or until golden brown. Drain, add to the sauce and stir to coat. Serve immediately.

Whether or not a tender pork ball surrounded by spinach leaves reminds you of a Lion's Head with its mane, this is a wonderful dish.

Lion's head pork balls

4 American servings
6 Chinese servings

1¼ pounds pork (ham or
    shoulder with a little fat)
4 dried Chinese mushrooms
6 water chestnuts, minced
1 clove garlic, crushed
2 thin slices fresh ginger root,
    minced
4 scallions, finely chopped
¼ teaspoon salt
⅛ teaspoon freshly ground
    pepper
½ teaspoon sugar
2 tablespoons sherry
1 teaspoon cornstarch
1 egg, lightly beaten
    Oil for deep frying

1 cup chicken or meat broth
4 tablespoons soy sauce
½ to ¾ pound spinach (or
    substitute Chinese cabbage)
1 tablespoon oil
2 teaspoons cornstarch
1 tablespoon water

Mince the pork. Soak the dried mushrooms in hot water for 20 minutes. Squeeze dry, cut off stalks and mince caps. Place pork and mushrooms in a bowl. Add water chestnuts, garlic, ginger root and scallions. Mix all of these ingredients with the salt, pepper, sugar, sherry, cornstarch and egg. Stir until ingredients are just mixed. Do not over mix or the mixture will become heavy. Divide into 4 to 6 portions and form each portion into a ball. Heat the oil for deep frying and fry the meat balls for about 3½ minutes or until lightly browned. Remove the meat balls, drain on paper towels and place them in a casserole. Heat the broth and soy sauce in a saucepan. Pour the broth over the meat balls and bring to a boil. Reduce heat, cover and simmer for about 20 minutes. Remove the heavy stems from the spinach and cut into 3 inch pieces. Heat 1 tablespoon oil in a wok, and stir fry spinach or cabbage for a few minutes to soften. Remove from the pan and place on top of the meat balls. Cover and simmer for about 10 more minutes. Remove the vegetable and place on a serving dish. Dissolve cornstarch in water and stir into the sauce to thicken. Place meat balls on vegetables. Cover with the sauce and serve immediately.

Szechuan style twice cooked pork

4 *American servings*
8 *Chinese servings*

  1 *pound fresh belly of pork*
    (fresh bacon)
1½ *quarts water*
  2 *tablespoons oil*
 ¼ *teaspoon salt*
  1 *clove garlic, crushed*
  2 *thin slices fresh ginger root,*
    minced
  1 *green pepper, seeded and cut*
    into thin strips
  2 *scallions, cut into ½ inch*
    pieces
  1 *tablespoon Chinese canned*
    brown bean sauce, mashed
 ½ *teaspoon sugar*
  1 *tablespoon sherry*
  1 *teaspoon hoisin sauce*
    combined with
  1 *teaspoon water*
 ⅛ *teaspoon cayenne pepper,*
    combined with
  1 *teaspoon oil*

Leave pork whole. Bring the
water to a boil and add pork.
Reduce heat, cover and simmer
for about 45 minutes to 1 hour.
Drain pork and cut into ¹⁄₁₆ to
⅛ inch thick slices.
Heat oil in wok or other pan.
Add salt, garlic and ginger root
and stir fry for 30 seconds. Add
pepper and scallions and stir fry
for 30 seconds. Add brown bean
sauce and stir fry for 1 more
minute. Add pork, sugar and
sherry and stir fry for 1½
minutes. Stir in hoisin sauce and
stir fry for another 1 to 1½
minutes. Stir in pepper-oil
mixture and serve.
Note: Originally, Szechuan
pepper oil was used and
sprinkled on just before serving.

Red pepper and oil are used as
substitutes here. Instead, a fresh
red chili-pepper, minced, can be
added with the green pepper.

GINGERROOT

Pork balls and broccoli

2 *American servings*
4 *Chinese servings*

  1 *recipe for deep fried pork*
    balls (see page 35)
  1 *pound fresh broccoli*
  2 *tablespoons oil*
 ½ *teaspoon salt*
  1 *clove garlic, peeled*
  1 *thin slice ginger root*
 ½ *cup chicken broth*
  1 *teaspoon soy sauce*
 ½ *teaspoon sugar*
  2 *teaspoons cornstarch*
  1 *tablespoon water*

Prepare pork balls according to
the directions in the recipe, but
deep fry for only 1 minute for
the second frying. Cut flowerets
from the broccoli. Discard lower
half of tough stems. Cut wide
stems in half lengthwise and
then cut diagonally into 2 inch
pieces. Parboil broccoli flowers
and stems in plenty of boiling
salted water for 4 minutes.
Drain and rinse under cold
running water until completely
cooled. Heat the oil in a wok or
skillet. Add salt and stir for 30
seconds. Add peeled clove of
garlic and ginger root. Stir fry
for 1 minute. Discard garlic and
ginger root. Add broccoli and
stir fry for 1 minute. Add pork
balls and stir fry for 1 minute.
Add chicken broth, soy sauce
and sugar and cook to heat
through. Stir in cornstarch
dissolved in cold water. Serve
immediately.

Stir fried pork kidneys

4 *American servings*
6 *Chinese servings*

  2 *pork or veal kidneys*
  1 *cup fresh peas, shelled (or*
    equal quantity canned peas)
  2 *tablespoons oil*
  4 *thin slices fresh ginger root,*
    shredded
  4 *whole scallions, cut in 1 inch*
    pieces
  4 *tablespoons soy sauce*
  2 *tablespoons sherry*
 ½ *teaspoon sugar*
  3 *tablespoons chicken or meat*
    broth
  2 *teaspoons cornstarch*
    dissolved in
1½ *tablespoons water*

Cut the kidneys in half and
remove fat and veins. Bring
plenty of salted water to the boil.
Drop in the kidneys and parboil
for 7 to 8 minutes. Rinse under
cold running water and drain or
wipe dry on paper towels. Cut
into ¼ inch thick slices. Place
fresh peas in a bowl and pour
boiling water over them. Leave
for 5 minutes and drain. Heat
2 tablespoons of the oil in a wok
or other pan. Add ginger root
and stir fry for 30 seconds.
Add kidneys and scallions and
stir fry for 1 minute. Stir in soy
sauce, sherry and sugar and stir
fry until sugar is dissolved. Add
peas and broth and bring to a
boil. Reduce heat a little, cover
and cook for 4 to 5 minutes.
Stir in cornstarch mixture to
thicken and serve. If canned peas
are used, add them only at the
last minute and stir to heat
through.

Beef

Stir fried beef in oyster sauce

2 American servings
4 Chinese servings

½ *pound flank steak, cut across the grain into slices ¼ inch thick and 2 inches long*
½ *teaspoon sugar*
1 *teaspoon cornstarch*
1 *teaspoon water*
2 *teaspoons cornstarch*
1 *tablespoon water*
2 *tablespoons oyster sauce*
½ *cup chicken or meat broth*
1 *tablespoon sherry*
2 *tablespoons soy sauce*
2 *tablespoons oil*
1 *thin slice fresh ginger root*
2 *whole scallions, finely chopped*
A few sprigs of parsley

Place the beef slices in a bowl. Add sugar, 1 teaspoon cornstarch and 1 teaspoon water and mix well. Combine remaining 2 teaspoons cornstarch with 1 tablespoon water. Combine oyster sauce, chicken or meat broth, sherry and soy sauce. Heat the oil in a wok or a skillet. Stir fry the ginger root in the oil for 1 minute until it is lightly browned. Discard the ginger root. Add the beef and stir fry for about 1½ minutes until it has lost any trace of red. Add scallions and stir fry another 30 seconds. Stir in oyster sauce mixture. Stir fry for 1 to 1½ minutes until hot. Stir in cornstarch mixture. Heat until thickened. Serve immediately garnished with parsley sprigs.

Stir fried shredded beef and celery

2 American servings
4 Chinese servings

½ *pound flank steak, sirloin steak or top rump of beef*
4 *stalks celery*
1 *large carrot*
½ *tablespoon sherry*
½ *tablespoon soy sauce*
½ *teaspoon sesame oil (optional)*
⅛ *teaspoon freshly ground pepper*
1 *teaspoon sugar*
2 *teaspoons cornstarch*
3 *tablespoons oil*
¼ *cup chicken broth*
1 *tablespoon cornstarch*
2 *tablespoons water*

Cut the beef across the grain into ⅛ inch thick slices and cut these slices into ½ inch wide strips. Cut celery stalks lengthwise into ¾ inch wide strips and then cut these strips into pieces 2 inches long. Slice the carrot crosswise into ⅛ inch thick rounds. Cut 16 of these rounds into a flower shape with a special cutter or a sharp knife. Discard the rest of the carrot. Combine sherry, soy sauce, sesame oil, pepper, sugar and cornstarch in a bowl. Add the beef and toss to coat. Let stand for about 10 minutes. Heat half of the oil in a wok or large skillet. Add the beef and stir fry for about 2 minutes. Remove beef from the pan and keep warm. Heat remaining oil, add celery and carrot flowers and stir fry for 1 minute. Add hot chicken broth and cook for 2 to 2½ minutes. Return beef to the pan and stir fry just to heat through. Mix cornstarch and water, add to the pan and stir until thickened. Serve immediately.

Stir fried beef, ginger and scallions

2 American servings
4 Chinese servings

½ *pound flank steak, sirloin steak or top rump of beef*
2 *tablespoons oil*
¼ *teaspoon salt*
6 *to 8 scallions, cut diagonally into 1 inch pieces*
8 *to 10 very thin slices fresh ginger root*
4 *tablespoons chicken or meat broth (recipes page 19)*
¼ *teaspoon sugar*
1 *teaspoon soy sauce*
2 *teaspoons cornstarch dissolved in*
1 *tablespoon water*

Cut beef across the grain in ⅛ to ¼ inch thick slices. Heat the oil in a wok or other pan. Stir fry the salt for about 1 minute. Add scallions and ginger root and stir fry 1 minute. Add beef and stir fry until it has lost any trace of red. Add broth, sugar and soy sauce and stir fry 1 more minute. Stir in cornstarch mixture to thicken and serve at once.

Carrots cut into flowers make an
attractive eye catcher in this dish
of shredded beef and celery,
(recipe page 39, 2nd column).

Fermented black beans add an interesting flavor to beef.

Beef balls are first rolled in shiny white glutinous rice and then steamed to savory tenderness, (recipe page 42, 1st column).

Stir fried beef in black bean sauce

4 American servings
6 Chinese servings

½ pound flank steak, sirloin steak or top round beef
1 tablespoon fermented black beans
2 small red peppers
1 small onion
3 tablespoons oil
1 clove garlic, crushed
2 thin slices fresh ginger root
1 tablespoon sherry
1 tablespoon cornstarch
½ cup chicken broth

Slice beef across the grain in ⅛ inch thick slices about 2 inches square. Soak fermented black beans in water for about 10 minutes. Drain and mash with the back of a spoon. Remove membranes and seeds from peppers and cut into 2 inch long and ¼ inch wide strips. Cut the strips into 1 inch diamonds. Cut onion in the same way. Heat 2 tablespoons of oil in a wok or large skillet and, when hot, add garlic and ginger root. Stir fry for 1 minute. Remove garlic. Add beef slices and stir fry for about 2 minutes. Remove from pan and keep warm. Add remaining oil and heat until hot. Add pepper and stir fry for about 2 minutes. Remove from pan and add to the beef. Add black beans to the pan and stir for about ½ minute. Mix sherry and cornstarch in a bowl until well blended. Pour chicken broth into the pan and heat quickly until boiling. Return beef and peppers and reheat. Stir in cornstarch mixture until thickened.

Steamed beef balls

4 American servings
6 Chinese servings

  1 cup uncooked long grain rice
  1 pound top round beef
  1 scallion, minced
  1 teaspoon finely minced fresh
    ginger root
  2 water chestnuts, minced
    (optional)
  1 egg, lightly beaten
  1 tablespoon soy sauce
½ tablespoon sherry
½ teaspoon salt
½ teaspoon sugar

Place the rice in a bowl, add
water to cover and soak for
about 1 to 1½ hours. Drain well
and spread out on a large plate
or rolling board. Remove all fat
and trimmings from beef and
mince the beef finely. Add
scallion, ginger root, water
chestnuts, egg, soy sauce, sherry,
salt and sugar and mix until
well blended. Form the mixture
into balls about 1½ inches in
diameter. Roll each ball in rice
until completely covered. Place
balls on a shallow, heatproof
dish, taking care that they are
½ inch or more apart from each
other. Place in a steamer and
steam for about ½ hour. Serve
immediately. They may be
dipped in soy sauce.

Stir fried beef and bean sprouts

4 American servings
8 Chinese servings

½ pound flank steak, sirloin
    steak or top rump of beef
  1 green pepper
  1 onion
  2 cups bean sprouts
½ tablespoon soy sauce
1½ tablespoons sherry
  1 tablespoon cornstarch
  4 tablespoons oil
  1 clove garlic, crushed
  2 thin slices fresh ginger root,
    minced
¼ teaspoon salt
  3 to 4 tablespoons chicken
    broth

Slice the beef across the grain
into ⅛-inch thick slices and cut
these slices into 2 inch long and
1-inch wide strips. Remove
membrane and seeds from green
pepper and cut into strips,
2-inches long and ¼-inch wide.
Halve the onion lengthwise
and then cut into long, thin
strips. If fresh bean sprouts are
used, blanch them in boiling
water for 30 seconds. Rinse
under cold running water and
drain. If canned bean sprouts
are used, put them in ice water
for ½ hour to restore their
crispness and drain. In a bowl,
mix soy sauce, sherry and
cornstarch until well blended.
Add the beef, toss to coat and
leave for about 10 minutes.
Heat half of the oil in a wok or
large skillet and, when hot, add
the beef. Stir fry for about
2 minutes, then remove from pan
and keep warm. Add remaining
oil and heat. Put garlic, ginger
root and salt into the pan and
stir fry for about 1 minute.
Remove garlic. Add pepper and
onion and stir fry for about
1 minute. Add bean sprouts and
stir fry for 1 more minute.
Pour in the chicken broth and
heat until boiling. Return the
beef and stir fry for 30 seconds
to reheat. Serve immediately.

Braised beef

4 American servings
8 Chinese servings

  3 tablespoons oil
  2 to 2½ pounds eye round or
    other pot roast of beef,
    cut into 1 inch cubes
½ cup soy sauce
  5 tablespoons sherry
  2 cups boiling water
  1 teaspoon sugar
    Freshly ground black pepper
  1 small onion, finely chopped

Heat the oil in a wok or a large, heavy pan. Stir fry the beef cubes until lightly browned. Add soy sauce and bring to a boil. Reduce the heat, cover and simmer 8 minutes. Add sherry and simmer, covered, 5 minutes. Add all the remaining ingredients and bring to a boil. Reduce heat, cover and simmer 1 hour or until very tender. The sauce, when strained, may be used as a starter for Master sauce (recipe page 82).

Red simmered beef

6 American servings
12 Chinese servings

2½ pounds eye round or pot
    roast of beef
  3 tablespoons oil
  1 clove garlic, crushed
  2 thin slices fresh ginger root,
    finely chopped
  6 tablespoons soy sauce
  4 tablespoons sherry
    Water to just cover the beef
  2 cloves star anise
  1 small piece cinnamon stick
¼ teaspoon freshly ground
    black pepper
½ teaspoon salt
  2 teaspoons sugar

Tie the meat at 2 inch intervals so that it will hold its shape while cooking. Heat the oil in a flame proof casserole. Brown the beef on all sides over high heat. Add all the remaining ingredients. Bring the liquid to a boil over high heat. Reduce the heat, cover the casserole and simmer for 1½ hours. Turn the beef every 30 minutes. Slice the beef and serve hot or cold with some of the sauce. The sauce can be refrigerated and kept for use in other dishes. If the sauce is heated to boiling point every 10 days, it will keep for several weeks. The beef can also be cut into 2 inch cubes before being added to the casserole. Reduce the cooking time to 50 minutes.

Steamed beef

2 American servings
4 Chinese servings

¾ to 1 pound flank steak,
    cut diagonally across the
    grain into ⅛ inch slices
  1 thin slice fresh ginger root,
    minced
  1 tablespoon soy sauce
½ tablespoon sherry
1½ teaspoons cornstarch
½ teaspoon salt
½ teaspoon sugar
  2 to 3 dried Chinese
    mushrooms
  2 scallions, minced
  1 teaspoon oil

Place the ginger root, soy sauce, sherry, cornstarch, salt and sugar in a bowl. Mix well. Add beef and toss to coat the strips. Set aside 20 minutes. Meanwhile, soak the mushrooms in warm water for 20 minutes. Squeeze dry and remove the stems. Mix the beef with the scallions. Oil a heat proof bowl and place the beef in it pressing down lightly. Top beef with the mushroom caps. Cover the bowl with aluminum foil, place in a steamer and steam 45 minutes to 1 hour.

Stir fried beef and cashew nuts

2 American servings
4 Chinese servings

½ pound flank steak, sirloin
    steak or top round steak
½ teaspoon sugar
  1 teaspoon cornstarch
  1 tablespoon soy sauce
½ cup meat broth or beef broth
  1 tablespoon soy sauce
½ teaspoon sesame oil
  1 tablespoon cornstarch
  2 tablespoons water
  3 tablespoons oil
  1 small onion, coarsely chopped
⅓ cup cashew nuts

Cut the beef across the grain into slices ¼ inch thick and 2 inches long. Place the beef in a bowl and combine with sugar, cornstarch and soy sauce. Combine meat broth, soy sauce and sesame oil. Mix cornstarch and water. Heat 2 tablespoons of oil in a wok or a skillet. Add beef and stir fry for 1½ minutes or until beef has lost any trace of red. Remove beef and add remaining oil. Heat the oil and add the onion. Stir fry onion for 45 seconds. Return beef to the pan. Add cashew nuts and stir fry 30 seconds to coat the nuts with oil. Add meat broth mixture and stir fry another 1½ minutes until heated through. Stir in cornstarch mixture to thicken into a sauce. Serve immediately.

Chicken

Stir fried chicken and mushrooms: a simple yet succulent dish, (recipe page 45, 1st column).

In China, duck and chicken are the favorite poultry, and duck is preferred over chicken. The Chinese have created many interesting ways of preparing duck, among which are drying, smoking and curing, though of course roasting, simmering and other cooking techniques are more frequently used in preparing duck. When only the poultry meat is used in a recipe, and the bird has been boned before it is cooked, the bones always go into the stock pot. Chicken and especially duck are sometimes briefly immersed in boiling water to get rid of the oil that is in the skin. It is also sometimes wiped with a hot, damp cloth. When buying fresh duck, be sure that the oil sacs that are situated above the tail have been removed because the oil could impart a disagreeable flavor to the dish. There are two interesting ways of treating duck before it is roasted. In some parts of China, air is inflated between the skin and the meat so that the skin separates from the meat. The duck is then roasted until it is very crisp. Such is the case with Peking duck for instance. It may also be filled with aromatic liquids (see the recipe for Cantonese roast duck). Chicken is very versatile and it can be used in combination with many other ingredients. As with pork and duck, a number of techniques can be combined to prepare one single chicken dish.

Chicken and mushrooms

2 American servings
4 Chinese servings

   1 whole chicken breast,
     skinned, boned and cut into
     ¼ inch cubes
½ teaspoon salt
⅛ teaspoon white pepper
   2 teaspoons cornstarch
   2 tablespoons oil
   1 thin slice fresh ginger root,
     minced
   1 cup small fresh button
     mushrooms
½ green pepper, seeded and cut
     into strips 1½ inches long
   2 teaspoons cornstarch
     dissolved in
   2 tablespoons chicken broth

Mix salt, pepper and cornstarch. Add chicken cubes and toss to coat. Heat the oil in a wok until very hot. Add ginger root and stir fry ½ minute. Add chicken and stir fry until all traces of pink have disappeared. Remove chicken from the pan. Add mushrooms and green pepper and stir fry 1½ minutes. Return chicken to the pan, add cornstarch mixture and stir until thickened. Serve immediately.

Braised chicken in soy sauce

4 American servings
6 Chinese servings

   1 (3 to 4 pound) chicken
¾ cup soy sauce
   3 tablespoons sherry
1½ cups chicken broth
½ tablespoon sugar
   3 tablespoons oil
   3 whole scallions, cut into
     1 inch pieces
   1 clove garlic, crushed and
     minced
   2 thin slices fresh ginger root,
     minced

Cut chicken through the bone with a cleaver into 2 inch pieces. Combine soy sauce, sherry, chicken broth and sugar. Bring liquid to boiling point. Cover the saucepan and remove from the heat. Heat oil in a wok or flame-proof casserole. Add chicken pieces and stir fry for 3 minutes until lightly browned on all sides. Add scallions, garlic and ginger root and stir fry for 1 minute. Add hot soy sauce mixture and return to boiling point. Reduce the heat. Cover and simmer for 40 minutes. Place chicken in a serving dish. Strain sauce and add a little of the sauce to the chicken.

Stir fried cooked chicken in oyster sauce

4 American servings
8 Chinese servings

  1 *(3 pound) chicken, cooked*
  2 *Chinese dried mushrooms*
  1 *small onion*
  3 *tablespoons oil*
  ½ *teaspoon salt*
  1 *clove garlic*
  1 *thin slice fresh ginger root*
  ¼ *cup chicken broth*
  2 *tablespoons soy sauce*
  1 *tablespoon sherry*
  2 *tablespoons oyster sauce*
  1 *teaspoon sugar*
  1 *tablespoon cornstarch*
  2 *tablespoons water*

Cut cooked chicken (through the bones) into 2 inch pieces. Soak dried mushrooms in hot water for 20 minutes, then squeeze dry. Cut off the stems and cut caps in ¼ inch wide strips. Cut onion into 1 inch pieces. Heat 2 tablespoons oil in a wok or other pan. Add salt, garlic and ginger root. Stir fry until lightly browned. Remove garlic and ginger root. Add chicken and stir fry for about 2 minutes or until well browned. Remove from the pan. Add remaining oil, heat and stir fry onion for about 1 minute. Return chicken to the pan. Add mushrooms, chicken broth, soy sauce, sherry, oyster sauce and sugar, and heat through. Dissolve cornstarch in water and stir in to thicken. Serve immediately.

Stir fried shredded chicken and bamboo

2 American servings
4 Chinese servings

  1 *whole chicken breast*
  2 *tablespoons oil*
  ¼ *teaspoon salt*
  2 *scallions, minced*
  ¾ *cup shredded bamboo shoots*
  4 *to 5 fresh mushrooms, sliced (optional)*
  ½ *cup chicken broth*
  1 *tablespoon soy sauce*
  ½ *teaspoon sugar*
  1 *tablespoon cornstarch dissolved in*
  3 *tablespoons water*

Remove skin and bones from chicken breast and shred meat. Heat 1 tablespoon oil in a wok or other pan. Add salt and stir fry for 30 seconds. Add chicken and stir fry until it has lost any trace of pink. Remove from pan. Add remaining oil, heat and stir fry scallions, bamboo shoots and mushrooms for 1 to 1½ minutes. Return chicken to the pan. Add chicken broth, soy sauce and sugar and simmer, covered, for another 1½ to 2 minutes. Stir in cornstarch to thicken and serve.

Chicken and nuts

2 American servings
4 Chinese servings

  3 *single chicken breasts*
  1 *tablespoon cornstarch*
  2 *tablespoons sherry*
  ½ *medium onion, finely chopped*
  2 *slices fresh ginger root, minced*
  1 *clove garlic, minced*
  3 *tablespoons soy sauce*
  1½ *tablespoons sherry*
  1 *teaspoon sesame oil*
  1 *teaspoon sugar*
  ¼ *cup chicken broth*
  3 *tablespoons oil*
  ¼ *cup roasted cashew nuts*
  1 *teaspoon cornstarch*
  1 *tablespoon water*

Remove the skin and bones from chicken breasts and cut breasts in ¾ inch cubes. Place the cubes in a small bowl and add 1 tablespoon cornstarch and 2 tablespoons sherry. Mix well. Combine the onion, ginger root and garlic. Combine soy sauce, sherry, sesame oil, sugar and chicken broth. Heat 2 tablespoons of the oil in a wok or a skillet. Add chicken and stir fry for 2 to 3 minutes until chicken is very lightly browned. Remove chicken from the pan. Add remaining 1 tablespoon of oil and heat until the oil is hot. Add onion, ginger root and garlic. Stir fry for 1 minute. Add cashew nuts and stir fry to coat with oil. Return chicken to the pan, add soy sauce mixture and stir fry to heat through. Mix remaining 1 teaspoon cornstarch with water and add to chicken. Stir 1 minute until sauce has thickened. Serve immediately.

Red simmered chicken

4 American servings
8 Chinese servings

  1 *(3 to 4 pound) chicken*
  1 *to 2 thin slices fresh ginger root, minced*
  1 *clove garlic, crushed*
  1 *tablespoon sugar*
  1 *to 2 cloves star anise*
  2 *tablespoons sherry*
  ½ *cup soy sauce*
  1 *tablespoon dark soy sauce (optional)*
  ½ *cup chicken broth or water*
  ½ *tablespoon sesame oil*
  6 *onion brushes (recipe page 20)*

Dry chicken thoroughly, inside and out, with paper towels. In a heavy casserole, combine all the remaining ingredients except the onion brushes. Bring to a boil and add the chicken. Reduce the heat, cover and simmer 1 to 1½ hours, turning the chicken every 15 minutes. Drain chicken and cut into 2 inch pieces. (You may also remove the meat from the bones and serve it moistened with a little of the sauce.) Decorate with onion brushes and serve. After straining, this sauce may be used as a Master sauce (recipe page 82) for other red simmered dishes.

In China, a chicken with its head and neck intact is used for this dish. The cavity is filled with more sherry and broth or water. The neck is tied closed and the other opening is trussed. The bird is then cooked by the same method, but for a shorter period of time.

White cooked chicken

4 American servings
8 Chinese servings

1 (4 pound) fresh chicken
  Water to cover
3 scallions
3 slices fresh ginger root
1 recipe soy-oil dip sauce or
1 recipe sherry-soy dip sauce
  (see page 83)

It is important that the chicken used for this dish is of the best quality available. As you will see, the flavor comes only from the chicken itself and not from any other ingredients. Place the whole chicken in a flame-proof casserole just large enough to hold it. Fill the casserole with enough water to cover the chicken. Remove the chicken and bring the water to boiling point. Cut scallions into pieces one inch long. Add scallions and ginger root slices to the water. Replace chicken in the casserole. When the water regains the boiling point, reduce the heat, cover the casserole and cook the chicken for 12 minutes. Turn the chicken, replace the lid and simmer another 10 minutes. Remove the casserole from the heat and allow the chicken to cool in the liquid. Cut the chicken legs and wings into 2 inch sections, cutting through the bone with a heavy cleaver. Arrange slices of breast meat in the center of a serving plate. Place the sections of wing, leg and thigh around the breast. Serve cold with soy-oil or sherry-soy dip sauce (see page 83).

Salt roasted chicken

3 American servings
6 Chinese servings

1 (3 pound) roasting chicken
3 thin slices fresh ginger root
1 scallion
¼ teaspoon salt
1 tablespoon sherry
  Coarse salt

Dip the chicken in boiling water and take it out at once. Wipe dry thoroughly inside and out. Cut the ginger slices in half and the scallion in 1 inch long pieces. Mix with the ¼ teaspoon salt and sherry and rub into the cavity of the chicken. Skewer or truss the chicken. In a casserole that is just big enough to hold the chicken comfortably, make a layer of salt about 1 to 1½ inches thick. Place the chicken on top and surround and top the chicken with a thick layer of salt. Remove the chicken and heat the measured salt in another heavy pan over medium heat, stirring occasionally, for about 45 minutes or until the salt is piping hot. Place a layer of hot salt in the casserole. Lay the chicken on it, breast-side down and surround and top it again with the remaining hot salt. Cover and cook over very low heat for 1 to 1¼ hours. Remove chicken and wipe off all excess salt. Remove skewers or trussing string and remove cavity seasoning. Serve hot or cold, cut into 2 inch pieces.

Deep fried chicken balls

2 American servings
4 Chinese servings

1 whole chicken breast, skinned, boned and coarsely ground
2 scallions, minced
1 tablespoon soy sauce
1 tablespoon sherry
1½ tablespoons cornstarch
¼ teaspoon salt
⅛ teaspoon sugar
1 egg, separated
  Oil for deep frying

Combine all the ingredients except the egg white and oil. Mix until thoroughly blended. Beat the egg white until stiff and fold into the chicken mixture. Chill 1 hour. Heat oil for deep frying until almost smoking. Form chicken mixture into small ovals and deep fry 4 or 5 at a time until golden brown. Remove with a slotted spoon and drain on paper towels. Serve with sweet sour sauce (recipes page 81 and 82).

Deep fried chicken

2 American servings
4 Chinese servings

1 young (2 pound) chicken
  Boiling water
2 teaspoons salt
¼ teaspoon freshly ground pepper
1 tablespoon sherry
½ teaspoon minced fresh ginger
  Oil for deep frying
8 onion brushes (recipe page 20)

Drop the chicken into boiling water and immediately lift it out. Wipe completely dry with clean towel. Mix salt, pepper, sherry and ginger and rub the chicken with this mixture inside and out. Heat the oil for deep frying until hot but not smoking (about 340 degrees on a deep frying thermometer). Lower chicken in a wire basket into the hot oil and deep fry for about 10 minutes, turning occasionally. Reduce heat to very low, lift out chicken and let cool for 6 to 8 minutes. Reheat oil, return chicken and deep fry for another 8 to 10 minutes or until golden brown and done. Lift out and drain well on paper towels. Arrange on a platter and garnish with onion brushes. Serve with a dip sauce made of 3 tablespoons sherry, 1 tablespoon soy sauce, 1 teaspoon chili sauce and ¼ teaspoon sugar, mixed until well blended.

Drunken chicken demonstrates the importance of wine and the versatility of chicken in Chinese cooking.

Drunken chicken

2 American servings
4 Chinese servings

  3 cups water
  1 whole scallion, cut in
     ½ inch lengths
  2 to 3 thin slices fresh ginger
     root, shredded
  1 whole chicken breast
  1 teaspoon salt
 ½ cup sherry

Bring the water to a boil in a saucepan and add scallion, ginger root and chicken breast. Reduce heat, cover the pan and simmer 15 minutes. Remove pan from the heat and leave 10 more minutes. Drain chicken and remove skin and bones, if any. Sprinkle breast on both sides with the salt, place in a bowl and add sherry. Cover with foil and refrigerate at least 1 day. To serve, drain breast and cut into bite sized cubes.

Poached chicken balls

4 American servings
8 Chinese servings

  1 recipe chicken velvet (recipe
     page 21)
  5 cups chicken broth
  1 tablespoon sherry
 ¼ teaspoon sugar
  1 tablespoon cornstarch,
     dissolved in
  2 tablespoons water

Chill prepared chicken velvet 2 hours before using in this recipe. In a saucepan, combine the broth, sherry and sugar and bring to a boil. Boil until the liquid has reduced to about 3 cups. Form the chilled chicken velvet into 1¼ inch balls. Moisten your hands with cold water before forming each ball. Reduce the heat so the liquid just simmers. Poach the balls 4 or 5 at a time for 1 to 2 minutes. Remove with a slotted spoon and drain on paper towels. Thicken the broth with the dissolved cornstarch. Place the balls on a heated serving dish, pour some of the sauce over and serve.

Steaming best preserves the rich, natural flavor of chicken, Chinese sausages or ham. Chinese mushrooms provide a colorful and savory contrast to the pure, white chicken meat.

Steamed chicken and sausages

3 American servings
6 Chinese servings

    1 *(2½ pound) chicken*
    2 *tablespoons sherry*
    ½ *teaspoon salt*
    2 *teaspoons cornstarch*
    2 to 3 *Chinese sausages, cut into thick diagonal slices*

With a cleaver, chop chicken into 2 inch pieces. Combine sherry, salt and cornstarch and toss chicken pieces in this mixture. Transfer chicken to a shallow dish and place sausage slices in between and on top of the chicken pieces. Place dish in a steamer and steam 45 minutes to 1 hour or until chicken is tender.

Steamed chicken and ham

3 American servings
6 Chinese servings

    2 *large chicken breasts, boned, but not skinned*
    2 to 3 *slices lean, smoked ham, cut ¼ inch thick*
    6 *large dried Chinese mushrooms*
    ½ *teaspoon salt*
    1 *tablespoon oil*
    1 *tablespoon sherry*

Cut chicken breasts crosswise into ⅓ inch thick slices with a very sharp knife. (Make sure the skin remains attached to the meat.) Cut the ham in as many slices as there are pieces of chicken and in approximately the same shape. Soak the mushrooms in hot water for 20 minutes. Squeeze dry carefully. Cut off the stalks and cut the caps in half. Sprinkle the chicken slices with salt and oil. Sprinkle the ham slices with sherry. In a shallow heatproof bowl, place rows of alternating chicken slices (skin side up) and ham slices. Surround with mushrooms halves or arrange mushrooms between chicken and ham. Steam for about 25 minutes or until tender. Serve hot.

Duck

Stir fried duck slices and bitter melon

4 American servings
6 Chinese servings

1 tablespoon fermented
  black beans
1 clove garlic, minced
1 (4 pound) duck
1 teaspoon soy sauce
2 teaspoons sherry
½ teaspoon salt
½ teaspoon sugar
2 teaspoons cornstarch
½ pound fresh bitter melon (or
  ½ of a 16 ounce can bitter
  melon) or substitute
  cucumber
4 to 6 tablespoons oil
1 cup chicken broth
2 teaspoons cornstarch
1½ tablespoons water

Soak black beans in water for
30 minutes. Drain and mash the
beans with the garlic. Cut the
duck meat from breast and
legs and reserve carcass for
making stock. Cut meat across
the grain in ⅛ to ¼ inch
thick slices. Mix soy sauce,
sherry, salt, sugar and
cornstarch. Add duck slices
and mix well. Leave for 20
minutes. When using fresh bitter
melon, wash and drain. Remove
stalks, cut bitter melon in half
lengthwise and remove seedy
center. Cut into ¼ inch slices.
Bring plenty of salted water to
a boil, add bitter melon and
parboil for 4 minutes.
Rinse under cold running water
until completely cooled. Drain.
When using canned bitter melon,
just drain off liquid, rinse under
cold running water, drain and
cut into slices. When cucumber
is substituted follow instructions,
for fresh bitter melon. Peel the
cucumber but do not parboil.
Heat half of the oil in a wok or
other pan. Add black bean
mixture and stir fry for 30
seconds. Add duck slices and
stir fry for about 2 to 2½
minutes or until lightly colored.
Remove from pan and keep
warm. Add remaining oil, heat
and stir fry the bitter melon
for 1 to 1½ minutes. Add broth
and bring to a boil. Return duck
slices to the pan, reduce heat,
cover and simmer for about
1½ to 2 minutes to heat
through. Mix cornstarch with
water and stir in to thicken.
Serve.

Braised duck with pineapple

6 to 8 American servings
6 to 8 Chinese servings

1 (4 pound) duck
6 slices canned pineapple
½ cup pineapple juice
1 clove garlic, crushed
2 thin slices fresh ginger root,
  minced
¼ teaspoon salt
3 tablespoons soy sauce
3 tablespoons sherry
1 teaspoon sugar
2 tablespoons oil
2 whole scallions, cut in ½
  inch pieces
3 cups boiling water
1 tablespoon cornstarch
  dissolved in
3 tablespoons water

Dip a clean cloth in hot water
and wring it out well. Wipe the
duck with the cloth. Cut
pineapple slices in half and
reserve ½ cup pineapple juice.
Prick the skin of the duck in
several places so the fat will
drain. Combine garlic, ginger
root and salt and rub the duck
with this mixture inside and
out. Leave for 10 minutes.
Mix the soy sauce with half of
the sherry and 1 teaspoon sugar
and brush the skin of the duck
with the mixture. Let stand 10
minutes and again brush the
duck with the mixture. Heat the
oil in a heavy casserole just
large enough to hold the duck
comfortably. Add the duck
and fry until nicely browned all
over. Discard the accumulated
fat. Add the water to the
casserole. Bring to a boil, reduce
heat, cover and simmer for
1 to 1¼ hours, turning every
15 minutes. Remove the duck
carefully and place on a serving
dish. Arrange halved pineapple
slices around the duck. Stir the
cornstarch mixture into the
duck broth to thicken. Pour
over duck and serve.

Cantonese roast duck

4 *American servings*
8 *Chinese servings*

1 *(4 pound) duck*
1 *teaspoon salt*
1 *piece dried tangerine peel*
2 *scallions, finely chopped*
2 *cloves garlic, minced*
2 *thin slices fresh ginger root,*
  minced
1 *tablespoon honey*
3 *tablespoons soy sauce*
1 *tablespoon sherry*
¼ *teaspoon cinnamon*
1 *to 1½ cups chicken broth*
3 *tablespoons honey*
2 *tablespoons soy sauce*
1½ *cups water*
1 *tablespoon vinegar*

Dry the cavity of the duck with paper towels. Rub the duck inside and out with salt and leave for 10 minutes. Soak the tangerine peel in hot water for 40 minutes. Drain the peel. Combine the peel, scallions, garlic, ginger root, honey, soy sauce, sherry, cinnamon and chicken broth in a saucepan. Heat to boiling point and then allow to cool for 5 minutes. Truss body cavity of duck securely. Place the duck in a bowl in which it can stand upright. Pour the hot liquid into the neck cavity and truss securely. (The liquid must be hot or the duck will "explode" in the oven.)
Place the duck on a roasting rack. Half fill the roasting tin with hot water. Roast the duck in a 400° oven for 20 minutes. Reduce the oven temperature to 325°. In the meantime, combine the remaining honey and soy sauce with water and vinegar. Baste the duck with this mixture and continue roasting the duck for 1½ to 1¾ hours basting every 15 minutes. Take the duck from the oven. Remove the trussing strings. Strain and reserve the liquid from the duck cavity. Chop the duck into 2 inch pieces, cutting through the bones with a heavy cleaver. Arrange the duck pieces on a serving dish. Spoon the liquid over the duck if it is served hot. However, do not add the liquid if the duck is to be served cold.
Note: Cold roast duck may be used in other stir fried dishes.

Stir fried roast duck and mixed meats

4 *American servings*
8 *Chinese servings*

1 *cup chicken broth*
1 *tablespoon soy sauce*
2 *tablespoons sherry*
¼ *teaspoon sugar*
1 *pound roast duck (previous*
  recipe)
¼ *pound roast pork*
3 *ounces cooked chicken*
¼ *pound lean smoked ham*
2 *cups water*
3 *ounces chicken livers*
½ *medium sized onion*
3 *tablespoons oil*
1 *clove garlic, crushed*
2 *thin slices fresh ginger root*
3 *scallions cut into ½ inch*
  slices
1 *tablespoon cornstarch*
  dissolved in
3 *tablespoons water*
  Few sprigs parsley

Combine broth, soy sauce, sherry and sugar in a saucepan. Bring to a boil, remove from the heat and keep warm. Cut duck, pork, chicken and ham into 2 inch long, ¾ inch wide and ¼ to ½ inch thick pieces. Bring 2 cups salted water to a boil and add the chicken livers. Reduce heat a little and cook for 5 to 6 minutes, or until firm, and cut into ¼ inch thick slices. Cut onion in ½ inch wide strips lengthwise. Heat the oil in a wok or other pan. Add garlic and ginger root and stir fry until lightly browned. Discard garlic and ginger. Add scallions and onion and stir fry for about 45 seconds. Add ham and stir fry for another minute, add chicken livers and stir fry for about 45 seconds. Then add roast duck, roast pork and chicken and stir fry to heat through. Pour in broth mixture and bring to a boil. Reduce heat and cook for ½ minute. Stir in cornstarch mixture to thicken. Transfer to a serving dish and garnish with parsley.
Shredded bamboo and bean sprouts (½ cup of each) may be added. They should be stir fried with the onion, then removed from the pan and added with the stock to heat through.

Fragrantly spiced and liquid filled Cantonese roast duck can be eaten as it is or transformed into stir fried roast duck with mixed meats, (recipe page 51, 1st column).

Red simmered duck

4 American servings
6 Chinese servings

2 *pieces dried tangerine peel*
1 *(4 pound) duck*
2 *thin slices fresh ginger root, minced*
6 *to 8 scallions, finely chopped*
6 *tablespoons soy sauce*
4 *tablespoons sherry*
¼ *teaspoon salt*
1 *clove star anise (optional)*
1 *teaspoon sugar*

Soak the tangerine peel in warm water for about 25 minutes and drain. Place the duck on its back in a heavy casserole or saucepan just large enough to hold it comfortably. Add water to cover and bring to a boil over medium heat. Cook for 3 to 4 minutes. Skim broth carefully. Add tangerine peel, ginger root, scallions, soy sauce, sherry, salt, star anise and sugar. Bring to a boil again, reduce heat, cover and simmer for about 50 to 60 minutes. Turn the duck over and simmer for another 30 to 40 minutes or until completely tender. Lift the duck from the casserole with a skimmer. Drain and cut the duck through the bone into 2 inch pieces with a cleaver. Strain the cooking liquid and serve a little of the liquid with the duck to moisten it. The remaining liquid can be used as a Master sauce (see page 82) for preparation of other red cooked dishes.

Fish

The crispness of this deep fried fish is set off by a delicious sweet sour sauce.

Deep fried whole fish and vegetables in sweet sour sauce

4 American servings
8 Chinese servings

- 1 (about 2½ pounds) sea bass or other whole fish
- 1 recipe sweet sour sauce II (recipe page 82)
- 1 medium onion
- 1 small green pepper
- 2 carrots
- 2 tablespoons oil
- ½ teaspoon salt
- 1 clove garlic, crushed
- 2 thin slices fresh ginger root, minced
- 4 fresh mushrooms, sliced ¼ inch thick
- ¼ cup shredded bamboo shoots (optional)
- 1 egg, beaten
   Flour or cornstarch
   Oil for deep frying

Have the fish cleaned and scaled and the head and fins removed. Ask the fishman to bone the fish but to leave the 2 sides of the fish attached at the tail. Carefully remove the skin and score the fish lightly on both sides. Prepare the sweet sour sauce but do not thicken it yet. Cut onion in half lengthwise and cut into 1 to 1½ inch pieces. Remove membranes and seeds from the pepper and cut into 1½ inch long and ½ inch wide strips. Cut carrots in a rolling cut, diagonally, into 1 inch pieces. Bring plenty of salted water to a boil, add carrots and parboil for about 4 to 5 minutes. Rinse under cold running water until completely cooled. Heat 2 tablespoons oil in a wok or other pan. Add salt and stir fry for about 30 seconds. Add garlic and ginger and stir fry for 1 minute. Discard garlic. Add onion, pepper, carrots, mushrooms and bamboo shoots and stir fry to coat with oil. Stir in reheated sweet sour sauce, cover and cook for about 1½ minutes. Remove from heat. Heat oil for deep frying. Brush the fish, inside and out, with beaten egg and dredge with flour or cornstarch. Deep fry the fish for about 6 minutes or until golden brown and tender. Remove fish with a skimmer and drain on paper towels. Bring sweet sour sauce to a boil and stir in cornstarch mixture to thicken. Place fish on a serving dish, pour over sauce and serve immediately.

The aim in cooking fish is to produce as natural a flavor as possible from the freshest fish available. Both fresh water and salt water fish are used and in comparison with the western style of cooking, more emphasis is placed on the fresh water varities. One aspect of fish cooking which seems strange to Western people is that cleaning and scaling are often the only preparations done ahead and, quite contrary to the general practice in the West, the fish is usually left whole, with the head, tail and fins still on. Leaving esthetic arguments aside, it is undoubtedly true that leaving the fish intact improves the flavor. Steaming as well as clear simmering are favorite ways of cooking fish because the subtle natural flavor is retained and the flesh is both tender and moist. However, deep frying, braising and even stir frying and pan frying are methods which are also used. Fish which is to be deep fried is either dredged in flour or cornstarch or is coated with a batter to seal in all of the juices. To eliminate the 'fishy' taste, a number of seasonings can be used with the fish. Ginger, garlic, scallions, black beans, soy sauce and wine are the most popular ingredients which are added. The fish is often scored to permit the flavors to be absorbed better and to expose a greater cooking surface.

For this recipe carp can be substituted by equal quantity sea bass, perch, trout or salmon.

Fried sole and peppers

3 American servings
6 Chinese servings

  1 pound flounder fillets
    (or substitute haddock or
    other firm, white fish)
  2 thin slices fresh ginger
    root, minced
  ½ teaspoon salt
  ¼ teaspoon sugar
  ½ teaspoon sesame oil
  1 tablespoon sherry
  1 small red pepper
  1 small green pepper
  1 medium onion
  1 egg, lightly beaten
  1 tablespoon cornstarch
  5 tablespoons oil
  1 slice fresh ginger root
  1 clove garlic
  1 teaspoon sherry
  1 teaspoon soy sauce

Cut sole fillets across the grain
into 1½ inch long pieces. Mix
minced ginger, salt, sugar,
sesame oil and sherry in a
bowl. Add the fish and marinate
for 2 hours. Cut peppers in half
lengthwise, remove membranes
and seeds and cut into 1½ inch
long diamond shapes, 1 inch
wide. Peel and cut the onion in
half lengthwise. Cut each half
into 1 inch wide sections.
Separate onion sections into
strips. Drain fish and wipe
dry with paper towels. Dip the
fish into egg to coat. Sprinkle
evenly with cornstarch. Heat
1 tablespoon of oil in a skillet
or large frying pan until quite
hot. Add ginger root and garlic
and let brown slightly. Remove
ginger and garlic, add pepper
and onion and stir fry for
about 1½ to 2 minutes over
medium heat. Add sherry and
soy sauce, stir and remove
all the ingredients from pan
and keep hot. Add remaining
oil and increase the heat. Add
the fish and fry until crisp and
golden on both sides. Remove
from pan and drain on paper
towels. Transfer to a serving
plate, add pepper and onion
mixture and serve immediately.

Deep fried sweet and sour fish

4 American servings
8 Chinese servings

  1 recipe sweet sour sauce I
    (recipe page 81)
  2 pounds fish fillets of any
    firm, white fish
  1 egg
  1 egg white
  2 to 2½ tablespoons cornstarch
  1 teaspoon salt
  1 teaspoon sherry
    Flour
    Oil for deep frying

Prepare sweet sour sauce as
directed and keep warm.
Cut fish fillets in ¾ to 1 inch
cubes. Mix egg, egg white,
cornstarch, salt and sherry into
a smooth batter. Dredge fish
very lightly in flour and lightly
coat with the batter. Heat the
oil for deep frying. Add fish
cubes, one at a time in several
batches. Deep fry until golden
brown. Remove from the pan
with a skimmer and drain on
paper towels. Transfer to a
serving dish. Pour sweet sour
sauce over and serve.

Braised carp and bean curd

4 American servings
8 Chinese servings

  1 (2 to 3 pound) carp or
  1 teaspoon salt
  1 tablespoon flour
  3 tablespoons oil
  2 thin slices fresh ginger root
  2 scallions, minced
  3 tablespoons soy sauce
  1 tablespoon sherry
  ⅛ teaspoon white pepper
  ½ to ¾ cup chicken broth
  1 teaspoon sugar
  ¼ teaspoon sesame oil or ½
    tablespoon oyster sauce
  1½ to 2 cakes bean curd, cut
    into 1 inch cubes

Have the fish man clean and
scale the fish. Remove head,
fins and tail, if desired. Wash
fish under cold running water,
drain and wipe dry with paper
towels. Make a few incisions
or scores on both sides. Sprinkle
with salt and set aside for 15
minutes. Sprinkle the fish
evenly with flour. Heat the oil
in a heavy pan just large enough
to hold the fish. Add the ginger
root and stir fry for 30 seconds.
Add the scallions and stir fry
for about 45 seconds. Add the
fish and fry over high heat until
brown on both sides. Sprinkle
with soy sauce, sherry and
pepper. Reduce the heat to
medium and cook for about
1½ minutes. Add chicken
broth, sugar and sesame oil or
oyster sauce and bring to a
boil quickly. Reduce heat,
cover and simmer for 8 to 10
minutes. Add bean curd to the
sauce and simmer for another
7 minutes. Serve immediately.

Simmered mullet

4 American servings
6 Chinese servings

2 small (¾ to 1 pound)
  mullets
2 teaspoons salt
6 cups water
2 scallions, minced
2 thin slices fresh ginger
  root, minced
2 tablespoons sherry
1 teaspoon salt
2 tablespoons oil

Have the fish cleaned and
scaled but leave head and tail
on. Score, sprinkle with the
salt on both sides and leave for
20 minutes. Rinse under cold
running water and drain.
Bring the water to a boil.
Add scallions, ginger root,
sherry, salt and oil to the water
and return to a rolling boil.
Place fish on a skimmer and
lower into the boiling liquid.
Reduce heat, cover and simmer
for 5 minutes. Turn off heat
completely and leave, covered,
for 20 to 25 minutes. Remove
the fish carefully and serve hot.

Steamed cod steak

4 American servings
8 Chinese servings

6 dried Chinese mushrooms
2 pounds cod steaks, 1½ to 2
  inches thick (or other firm
  white fish)
½ teaspoon salt
2 slices fresh ginger root,
  minced
2 tablespoons soy sauce
1 tablespoon oil

Soak the mushrooms in warm
water for 20 minutes. Squeeze
dry, remove stalks and leave
caps whole. Place fish and
mushroom caps in a shallow
heatproof dish and sprinkle
with salt. Combine ginger root
with soy sauce and oil. Sprinkle
over fish. Place fish in a
steamer and steam for about
15 minutes. Remove from
steamer and serve immediately.

Fish balls

6 American servings
10 Chinese servings

2 pounds raw fish fillets, such
  as flounder, cod or haddock
2 thin slices fresh ginger root
6 to 8 tablespoons water
1 tablespoon sherry
2 tablespoons minced onion
  or scallion
½ teaspoon salt
2 egg whites
1 teaspoon cornstarch

Mince or grind the fish and
place in a bowl. Chop the ginger
root and, using a garlic press,
squeeze the juice over the fish.
Beat the fish until smooth,
adding half of the water
gradually. Add sherry, onion
and salt. Beat until well blended.
Add the egg whites and the
cornstarch and beat vigorously
for 1 minute. Continue beating
for another few minutes,
adding more water gradually if
the mixture seems very stiff.
Divide the mixture into 4
equal parts and form each part
into 5 small balls. Bring 1½ to 2
quarts of water to a boil.
Reduce heat a little, drop in
the fish balls and poach them
for about 6 minutes. Remove
them with a skimmer and use as
directed in recipes. If they are
not to be used immediately,
drop them into cold water and
refrigerate until used.

Fish balls in bouillon

6 American servings
10 Chinese servings

1 recipe fish balls (see
  previous recipe)
2 cups chicken broth
1 tablespoon sherry
½ teaspoon salt
2 egg yolks
1 scallion, minced or 2
  tablespoons chopped chives

Prepare fish balls as described
in previous recipe and reserve
the egg yolks used in this
preparation. Poach the fish
balls and drain. Bring chicken
broth to a boil. Add sherry
and salt. Reduce the heat a
little, add the fish balls and heat
through. Remove from the heat,
stir in egg yolks and sprinkle
on the scallion or chives.
Serve immediately.

Braised eel and crisp roast pork is an exciting new way to fish for compliments.

Braised eel and crisp roast pork

4 American servings
6 Chinese servings

½ recipe crisp roast belly of
  pork (recipe page 34)
2 pounds eel, cleaned and
  skinned
4 tablespoons oil
¼ teaspoon salt
2 scallions, finely chopped
2 thin slices fresh ginger
  root, minced
1¼ cups water or chicken broth
3 tablespoons soy sauce
1 tablespoon sherry
1 teaspoon brown sugar
1 tablespoon cornstarch
2 tablespoons water

Prepare the crisp roast pork
as directed in recipe on page 34.
Cut eel into pieces 2 inches
long. Heat oil in a heavy pan
or heatproof casserole dish.
Add salt, scallions and ginger
root and stir fry for about 1
minute. Add eel and stir fry
for another minute. Add water
or broth, soy sauce and sherry
and bring to a boil. Reduce
heat, cover and simmer for
about 10 to 12 minutes. Stir in
sugar, add pork and simmer
for about 2 to 4 minutes more
to heat through. Meanwhile
dissolve cornstarch in water
and stir in to thicken. Serve hot.

The Steamed sea bass recipe is originaly prepared with carp. Fragrant steamed carp is surrounded by refreshing onion brushes.

The Steamed sea bass recipe is originaly prepared with carp. Fragrant steamed carp is surrounded by refreshing onion brushes.

Steamed sea bass

6 American servings
10 Chinese servings

- 1 (3 pound) sea bass or other firm fish
- 1 teaspoon salt
- 1½ to 2 tablespoons fermented black beans
- 1 clove garlic, crushed
- 2 thin slices ginger root, shredded
- 2 scallions, minced
- 3 tablespoons soy sauce
- 1 tablespoon sherry
- ½ teaspoon sugar
- 1 tablespoon oil
- 6 onion brushes (recipe page 20)

Have the fish cleaned and scaled but left whole with head and tail on. Score crosswise on both sides and sprinkle with salt. Soak the fermented black beans in water for about 20 minutes. Drain and mash together with the garlic. Place fish in a shallow heatproof dish. Mix all ingredients except onion brushes until blended and spread over fish. Place in a steamer and steam for 30 to 35 minutes or until done. Remove from steamer. Decorate with onion brushes and serve.

Shrimp, crab and other seafood

Besides fish, the Chinese also eat a great deal of other seafood including shrimp, crab, lobster, scallops, clams and oysters. They are also fond of sea cucumber, squid and sea urchins. Prolonged

Stir fried lobster and pork

3 American servings
6 Chinese servings

> 1 live (2 pound) lobster
> 1 cup (6 ounces) lean pork
> 1 clove garlic, minced
> 1 thin slice fresh ginger root, minced
> 2 tablespoons soy sauce
> 1 tablespoon sherry
> ½ teaspoon salt
> ¼ teaspoon sugar
> ⅛ teaspoon sesame oil
> 3½ tablespoons oil
> 4 tablespoons chicken broth
> 1 tablespoon cornstarch
> 2 tablespoons water
> 1 egg, lightly beaten

Kill the lobster by inserting the point of a sharp knife between the body and the tail. Place the lobster on its back on a chopping board. Chop lobster with a heavy cleaver down its entire length. Chop tail into 2 inch pieces. Cut legs in half and chop each claw into 3 pieces. Reserve the coral and tomalley and mash together in a small bowl. Mince the pork finely. Place the pork in a bowl and add garlic, ginger root, soy sauce, sherry, salt, sugar and sesame oil. Mix the cornstarch and water. Heat the oil in a wok or a skillet. Add the lobster and stir fry about 2½ minutes until the shell is bright red and the lobster meat is white and opaque. Remove the lobster. Add the pork mixture and stir fry for 2 minutes until pork has lost any trace of pink. Return lobster to the pan. Add chicken broth and heat to boiling point. Add cornstarch paste and heat 30 seconds until the sauce has thickened. Stir in egg and stir fry 30 seconds. Serve immediately.

Stir fried shrimp, onion and bean sprouts

4 American servings
8 Chinese servings

> 1 pound small shrimp, peeled
> 1 medium onion
> 2 scallions
> 2 slices fresh ginger root
> 1 cup chicken broth
> ½ tablespoon soy sauce
> 1 tablespoon sherry
> 1½ teaspoons sugar
> 1 tablespoon cornstarch
> 2 tablespoons water
> 2 tablespoons oil
> ½ cup bean sprouts

Wash shrimp and drain thoroughly. Cut onion in half lengthwise, then in half crosswise and then shred lengthwise. Cut the scallions in ½ inch long pieces. Mince the ginger root finely. Place chicken broth, soy sauce, sherry and sugar in a saucepan. Bring to a boil, remove from heat and keep warm. Dissolve cornstarch in water. Heat the oil in a wok or other pan. Add the ginger and stir fry for 30 seconds. Add the shrimp and scallion and stir fry for 1½ minutes. Add bean sprouts and stir fry for another 1 minute. Stir in hot chicken broth mixture and bring quickly to a boil. Stir in cornstarch mixture to thicken and serve immediately.

Deep fried shrimp

4 American servings
6 to 8 Chinese servings

> 1½ pounds large shrimp

Batter:

> 3 tablespoons flour
> 1 tablespoon cornstarch
> 1 egg, lightly beaten
> 1 teaspoon salt
> ½ teaspoon sugar
> 1 teaspoon sherry
> 4 tablespoons water

Sauce:

> 3 tablespoons soy sauce
> 3 tablespoons tomato sauce
> 1 teaspoon brown sugar
> 1 teaspoon lemon juice
> ¼ teaspoon tabasco sauce
>
> Oil for frying
> 6 onion brushes (recipe page 20)
> ½ cup plum sauce (recipe page 83)
> ¼ cup salt and pepper mix (recipe page 83)

Shell and devein the shrimp leaving the tail intact. Combine the batter ingredients and beat until smooth. Mix the sauce ingredients until well blended. Heat the oil for deep frying. Dip the shrimp into the batter to coat lightly and drop them into the hot oil one by one. Fry until golden brown and drain on paper towels. Arrange the shrimp on a platter in a circle with the tails pointing outward. Place the onion brushes in the center. Serve with the sauces and salt and pepper mix on the side.

cooking tends to make seafood both tough and unpalatable, so the number of techniques used for cooking it are generally restricted to stir frying, deep frying, pan frying and steaming. Though

fresh seafood is generally preferable, either canned or frozen seafood can be used if necessary. Products such as canned abalone need only be heated very briefly. Special care

which needs to be taken in preparing various types of seafood is given in the recipes. Scallops, squid, abalone, shrimp and oysters are also sold dried in Chinese food stores.

Deep fried shrimp and sweet sour sauce

4 American servings
8 Chinese servings

  1 pound large shrimp
  1 recipe sweet sour sauce III
    (recipe page 82)
  3 tablespoons flour
  ½ tablespoon cornstarch
  1 egg
  ½ teaspoon salt
  ½ teaspoon sherry
  ½ teaspoon minced ginger root
  3 tablespoons water
    Oil for deep frying

Shell the shrimp and take out black vein. Cut shrimp into 1 to 1½ inch pieces. Prepare the sweet sour sauce and keep warm. Mix flour, cornstarch, egg, salt, sherry, ginger root and water into a smooth batter. Heat the oil for deep frying. Dip shrimp pieces in the batter to coat lightly and deep fry, dropping them in the hot oil one by one, for about 3 minutes or until floating and golden brown. Drain on paper towels. Transfer to a serving dish. Serve with hot sweet sour sauce.

Stir fried shrimp, chicken livers and vegetables

3 American servings
8 Chinese servings

  1 pound giant shrimp
  ½ cup shelled fresh peas or
    frozen peas
  1 scallion
  3 tomatoes
  1 cup chicken broth
  1 tablespoon soy sauce
  1 tablespoon sherry
  1 tablespoon cornstarch
  3 tablespoons water
  3 tablespoons oil
  1 clove garlic, crushed
  2 thin slices fresh ginger
    root, minced
  ½ teaspoon salt
  1 teaspoon sugar

Shell the shrimp and take out the black vein. Cut the shrimps in half lengthwise. Shell the fresh peas. Place fresh or frozen peas in a bowl, pour boiling water over them and let stand for 4 minutes. Drain thoroughly. Cut the scallion in ½ inch long pieces. Peel, seed and drain the tomatoes and cut into wedges. Place chicken broth, soy sauce and sherry in a saucepan and bring to a boil. Remove from the heat and keep warm. Mix the cornstarch with the water. Heat 2 tablespoons oil in a wok or other pan. Add garlic, ginger root and scallion and stir fry for 1 minute. Add shrimp and stir fry for about 1½ minutes. Remove from pan. Add remaining oil and heat. Add salt and stir fry for another ½ minute. Add sugar and chicken broth mixture and bring quickly to the boil.

Return shrimp and scallion to the pan and heat through for about 1 minute. Stir in cornstarch mixture to thicken and serve immediately.

Deep fried shrimp balls

4 American servings
6 Chinese servings

  1½ pounds large shrimp
  2 ounces pork fat (¼ cup
    minced)
  4 to 5 water chestnuts
  1 scallion, minced
  1 thin slice fresh ginger root,
    minced
  1 egg
  1 tablespoon cornstarch
  ½ teaspoon salt
  1 tablespoon sherry
    Oil for deep frying
  6 slices lemon
    Few sprigs parsley

Shell the shrimp and take out the black vein. Mince shrimp together with the pork fat and water chestnuts. Combine shrimp mixture with scallion, ginger, egg, cornstarch, salt and sherry until smooth and well blended. Form into balls about 1½ inches in diameter. Heat oil for deep frying. Deep fry shrimp balls, a few at a time, for about 2½ minutes or until golden brown. Drain on paper towels. Transfer to a serving dish, decorate with lemon slices and parsley.

Shrimp combines surprisingly well with meats in this stir fried shrimp and chicken liver dish, (recipe page 59, 2nd column).

Deep frying makes shrimp balls a tantalizing crisp, golden brown delicacy, (recipe page 59, 4th column).

Stir fried crab and mushrooms

2 American servings
4 Chinese servings

1 *(6 to 8 ounce) can crabmeat*
   Liquid from the can
½ *cup small button*
   mushrooms
2½ *tablespoons oil*
½ *teaspoon salt*
1 *clove garlic, crushed*
1 *scallion, minced*
1 *tablespoon sherry*
1 *tablespoon cornstarch*
   dissolved in
4 *tablespoons water*

Drain canned crabmeat and reserve liquid. Pick over crabmeat and remove cartilage. Wash and trim mushrooms, leaving whole if small or cutting in half if larger. Heat 1½ tablespoons oil in a wok. Add salt and garlic and stir fry for 1 minute. Discard garlic and add mushrooms and scallion. Stir fry for about 3 minutes. Remove from pan. Heat remaining oil, add crabmeat and stir fry for 1 minute or just to heat through. Add sherry and can liquid and stir to heat through. Return mushrooms and scallion to the pan, stir in the cornstarch mixture to thichen and serve immediately.
Note:
If available, canned Chinese mushrooms can be used instead of button mushrooms. They are succulent and certainly improve the dish.

Stir fried crab, ginger and scallions

3 American servings
6 Chinese servings

  2 large live crabs
  1 clove garlic
  3 thin slices fresh ginger root
  3 to 4 scallions
  2 tablespoons oil
  ½ to ¾ cup chicken broth
  1 tablespoon soy sauce
  1 tablespoon sherry
  ½ teaspoon salt
  ¼ teaspoon sugar
  ⅛ teaspoon sesame oil
  1 tablespoon cornstarch
    dissolved in
  2 tablespoons water
  1 egg, lightly beaten

Wash the crabs in water.
Bring plenty of water to a boil.
Drop in the crabs and boil
for about 25 minutes. Drain
and let cool. Twist off claws
and legs and crack the legs.
With a chopping knife or
cleaver, chop claws in half and
crack. Separate the body from
the shell and discard all soft,
spongy parts. Chop body into
large pieces. Crush the garlic
and mince the ginger root.
Cut the scallions into ½ inch
pieces. Heat the oil in a wok
or other pan. Add garlic and
ginger root and stir fry for
1 minute. Discard garlic. Add
scallions and stir fry for ½
minute. Add crab pieces and
stir fry to coat with oil. Pour in
broth, soy sauce, sherry, salt,
sugar and sesame oil and bring
quickly to a boil. Stir in the
dissolved cornstarch to thicken.
Add the egg and stir fry ½
minute. Serve immediately.

Stir fried squid and vegetables

4 American servings
6 Chinese servings

  2 dried Chinese mushrooms
  1 pound small squid, cleaned
  1 cup Chinese cabbage or
    celery cabbage
  1 small onion
  2 thin slices fresh ginger root
  ½ cup chicken broth
  1 tablespoon soy sauce
  ½ teaspoon sugar
  2 teaspoons cornstarch
  1 tablespoon water
  3 tablespoon oil
  ½ teaspoon salt

Soak dried mushrooms in hot
water for about 20 minutes.
Squeeze dry, remove stems and
cut caps in ½ inch wide strips.
Rinse squid under cold water.
Cut off and reserve the
tentacles and cut bodies in
half lengthwise. Score squid
lengthwise and crosswise at
¼ to ½ inch intervals and then
cut along the scores in 1½ by
½ inch strips. Cut cabbage into
2 inch long and ¾ inch wide
pieces. Parboil cabbage for
3 minutes in boiling salted
water. Rinse cabbage under
cold running water and drain.
Halve the onion lengthwise
and then cut into small strips
lengthwise. Mince ginger root.
Mix broth, soy sauce and sugar
in a bowl. Dissolve cornstarch
in water. Heat the oil in a
wok or other pan. Add the salt
and stir fry for 30 seconds.
Add the squid pieces and
tentacles and stir fry for about
1 minute. Add onion, stir fry
for 30 seconds, then add
ginger root, cabbage and

mushrooms and stir fry to
coat with oil. Add chicken
broth mixture and bring to a
boil. Reduce heat, cover and
cook for about 3 minutes.
Stir in cornstarch to thicken
and serve.
Note: Scoring the squid shortens
the cooking time and makes
the pieces curl up in an
attractive way.

Stir fried abalone

3 American servings
6 Chinese servings

  6 small dried Chinese
    mushrooms
  1 (16 ounce) can abalone
  1 small onion
  3 tablespoons oil
  ½ teaspoon salt
  ¼ cup chicken broth
  4 tablespoons abalone liquid
    from the can
  1 tablespoon sherry
  ¼ teaspoon sesame oil
  1 tablespoon cornstarch
    dissolved in
  2 tablespoons water

Soak the dried Chinese
mushrooms in hot water for
20 minutes. Squeeze the
mushrooms dry. Cut off the
stems and leave the caps whole.
Drain the abalone and reserve
4 tablespoons of the liquid
from the can. Cut the abalone
into slices ¼ inch thick.
Cut the onion in half lengthwise
and then into 1 inch long and
½ inch wide strips. Heat the
oil in a wok or skillet. Add the
salt and stir fry for 30 seconds.
Add the mushroom caps and
onion. Stir fry for 1½ minutes.
Add the chicken broth,
abalone liquid, sherry and
sesame oil. Bring to boiling
point. Add the abalone and
bring the mixture to boiling
point quickly. (Do not cook
the abalone too long or it will
toughen.) Stir in the cornstarch
paste to thicken the sauce.
Serve immediately.

Stir fried oysters

2 American servings
4 Chinese servings

  2 teaspoons soy sauce
  1 teaspoon cornstarch
12 oysters, shucked
  1 cake bean curd
  1 clove garlic, crushed
  1 slice fresh ginger root,
    minced
¼ teaspoon salt
  2 tablespoons soy sauce
  2 tablespoons sherry
  4 tablespoons chicken broth
    or water
  1 teaspoon cornstarch
    Oil for deep frying
  2 tablespoons oil
  2 slices fresh ginger root,
    shredded
  4 whole scallions, cut into
    ½ inch strips
  2 tablespoons ham garnish
    (recipe page 21)

Combine 2 teaspoons soy sauce and 1 teaspoon cornstarch in a small bowl. Add the oysters and coat them with the mixture. Let stand 10 minutes. Cut the bean curd into strips ½ to ¾ inch long. Combine garlic, ginger root and salt. Gently toss the bean curd in this mixture and let stand 5 minutes. In a small bowl, combine the soy sauce, sherry, chicken broth and 1 teaspoon cornstarch. Heat oil for deep frying. Carefully wipe off the garlic and ginger clinging to the bean curd. Fry the pieces of bean curd until golden brown and crisp on the outside but tender inside. Drain on paper towels. Heat 2 tablespoons oil in a wok. Add shredded ginger root and scallions and stir fry 1 to 1½ minutes. Add oysters with their liquid and stir fry 1½ to 2 minutes. Remove oysters from the wok. Add soy sauce mixture and bring to a boil. Add bean curd and heat 1 minute. Return oysters to the wok and heat briefly. Transfer to a serving dish and sprinkle with ham garnish.

Stir fried scallops and bamboo

4 American servings
8 Chinese servings

  1 pound scallops
¾ cup bamboo shoots
  2 cakes bean curd
  2 tomatoes
  1 scallion
  1 clove garlic
  3 tablespoons oil
½ teaspoon salt
  1 tablespoon soy sauce
½ tablespoon sherry
½ teaspoon sugar
¼ cup chicken broth
⅛ teaspoon sesame oil
  2 teaspoons cornstarch
  1 tablespoon water

Cut scallops in ¼ inch thick slices. Cut bamboo shoots into slices 1 inch long, ½ inch wide and ⅛ to ¼ inch thick. Cut bean curd cakes in half and then crosswise into ¼ to ½ inch thick slices. Peel, seed and drain tomatoes. Mince scallion and garlic. Heat 2 tablespoons oil in a wok or other pan, add scallops and stir fry for about 1 to 1½ minutes. Remove from pan and keep warm. Add 1 tablespoon oil, heat and add salt and garlic. Stir fry for 30 seconds. Add bean curd and stir fry gently for about 2 minutes or until lightly browned. Add bamboo and stir fry for another ½ minute. Add soy sauce, sherry, sugar and tomatoes and stir fry for 30 seconds. Return scallops to the pan and stir fry to heat through. Add broth and bring quickly to a boil. Mix sesame oil, cornstarch and water and stir in to thicken. Serve immediately.

Stir fried scallops and chicken livers

2 American servings
4 Chinese servings

½ pound chicken livers, cleaned
½ cup chicken broth
  2 tablespoons soy sauce
  1 tablespoon sherry
¼ teaspoon sugar
  2 tablespoons oil
¾ pound scallops, sliced ¼
    inch thick
  1 thin slice fresh ginger root,
    minced
  2 whole scallions, minced
½ tablespoon cornstarch
    dissolved in
1½ tablespoons water

Place chicken livers in a bowl. Cover with boiling water and let stand 3 to 4 minutes. Drain, dry carefully on paper towels and set aside. Combine the chicken broth, soy sauce, sherry and sugar in a small bowl. Heat the oil in a wok. Add scallops and stir fry 2 minutes. Remove from the pan. Add ginger and scallions and stir fry ½ minute. Add livers and stir fry 2 minutes. Add chicken broth mixture and bring to a boil. Stir in the cornstarch mixture to thicken. Return scallops to the wok and heat through. Serve immediately.

Egg dishes

Shiny brown soy eggs and marbled tea eggs show the fascinating ways the Chinese have with eggs, (recipe page 67, 3rd column).

It is not difficult to see why Crab Foo Young is a very popular dish in China and abroad once you have made it yourself.

Crab foo young

Plain boiled or fried eggs, are seldom eaten in China. Usually they are seasoned one way or another when boiled, and are combined with numerous other ingredients when steamed, scrambled or fried. Lard is sometimes used as a cooking agent in the preparation of eggs. Eggs are frequently served as a garnish in soups or with other dishes. They play an important role in fried rice dishes and are used in batters for deep fried foods.

3 American servings
6 Chinese servings

4 eggs
½ teaspoon salt
⅛ teaspoon freshly ground pepper
2 teaspoons sherry
1 cup fresh or canned crabmeat
3 to 3½ tablespoons oil
2 scallions, minced
6 medium sized mushrooms, sliced
1 tablespoon finely chopped chives
1 recipe Foo Young sauce (see page 82)

Beat the eggs lightly in a bowl. Stir in salt, pepper and sherry. Shred the crabmeat and remove any hard pieces. Heat 1½ tablespoons oil in a wok or frying pan. Stir fry scallions, mushrooms and chives for 2 minutes over moderate heat. Add crabmeat and stir fry for 1 more minute over high heat. Remove the pan from the heat and allow the mixture to cool for a few minutes. Add the egg mixture. Heat 2 tablespoons of oil in a wok or frying pan with sloping sides. Add the crab and egg mixture and cook the omelette until just set and lightly browned on the underside. Fold the omelette and continue cooking for 1 minute. Place omelette on a serving plate. Serve immediately with Foo Young sauce.

Note: A few choice pieces of crabmeat may be reserved to decorate the omelette.

Chicken omelet

Shrimp foo young

3 American servings
6 Chinese servings

  1 *dried Chinese mushroom*
    Breast of ½ a small
    chicken, skinned, boned
    and shredded
 ¼ *teaspoon salt*
1½ *teaspoons cornstarch*
  3 *tablespoons oil*
  1 *scallion, minced*
  5 *thin slices bamboo*
    shoot, shredded
  1 *tablespoon ham garnish*
    (recipe page 21)
  2 *tablespoons chicken broth*
  5 *eggs*
 ½ *teaspoon salt*
    Freshly ground black pepper
  1 *tablespoon finely chopped*
    chives

Soak the mushroom in warm water for 20 minutes. Remove and discard the stem and shred the cap. Mix the chicken with the salt and cornstarch. Heat 1 tablespoon oil in a wok or frying pan with sloping sides. Add chicken and stir fry for 1 or 2 minutes or until all traces of pink disappear. Remove chicken from the pan. Add 1 more tablespoon oil and stir fry scallion, bamboo shoot, ham and mushroom 2 minutes. Return chicken to to the pan and add broth, scraping up the browned bits clinging to the pan. Remove mixture from the pan and wipe the pan out with paper towels. Beat the eggs with the salt, pepper and chives. Add the chicken mixture and stir to combine. Heat the remaining 1 tablespoon oil in the pan

until very hot. Pour in the omelette mixture and stir with a fork until the eggs begin to set. Lift the edge of the omelette so that the uncooked egg will run under the cooked part. With the aid of a large spatula, fold the omelette in half. Serve immediately.

3 American servings
6 Chinese servings

  4 *eggs*
 ½ *teaspoon salt*
 ⅛ *teaspoon freshly ground*
    pepper
  2 *teaspoons sherry*
  3 *to 3½ tablespoons oil*
  2 *scallions, shredded*
  1 *tablespoon finely shredded*
    bamboo shoots
  1 *cup peeled small shrimp*
  1 *cup bean sprouts, loosely*
    packed
 ½ *tablespoon soy sauce*
  1 *recipe Foo Young sauce*
    (recipe page 82)

Beat eggs lightly in a bowl and stir in salt, pepper and sherry. Heat 1 to 1½ tablespoons oil in a wok or large frying pan and stir fry scallions and bamboo shoots for 1½ minutes. Add shrimp, bean sprouts and soy sauce and stir fry for another 1 minute. Remove from heat, let cool for a few minutes, then stir into egg mixture. Heat 2 tablespoons oil in a frying pan, with sloping sides. Add the egg mixture and cook the omelette until set and lightly browned on the underside. Fold the omelette and continue cooking for a few seconds. Invert the omelette onto a serving dish. Serve with Foo Young sauce (recipe page 82).
Note: A few shrimp may be reserved to decorate the omelette.

Scrambled eggs with pork, onion and chives

3 American servings
6 Chinese servings

  5 eggs
  1 teaspoon water
  ½ teaspoon salt
  ⅛ teaspoon white pepper
  2 tablespoons finely chopped chives
1½ tablespoons oil
  2 slices fresh ginger root
  1 scallion, minced
  1 medium onion, shredded lengthwise
  ½ cup shredded lean pork
  1 tablespoon ham garnish (recipe page 21)

Combine eggs, water, salt, pepper and chives in a bowl and beat until well blended. Heat oil in a frying pan until very hot. Add ginger root and stir fry 1 minute. Remove ginger root from the pan and add scallion and onion. Stir fry ½ minute. Add pork and stir fry 2 minutes. Reduce the heat and add the eggs. Stir as for scrambled eggs until soft curds form. Serve immediately topped with ham garnish.

Soy colored eggs

4 American servings
4 Chinese servings

  4 eggs
  ½ cup soy sauce
  ½ cup chicken broth or water
  6 tablespoons sugar
  ¼ teaspoon sesame oil
  1 tablespoon minced onion
16 to 20 radishes
     Plum sauce (see page 83)

Place the eggs in a saucepan. Cover with cold water and boil gently for 5 minutes. Remove from the heat and put under cold running water for 5 minutes. Remove the shells carefully. Place the soy sauce, chicken broth, sugar, sesame oil and onion in a small saucepan. Bring the mixture to boiling point. Add the eggs, cover the pan and simmer for 10 minutes. Remove from the heat and allow the eggs to cool in the sauce for 30 minutes. Turn the eggs during the cooking and cooling to ensure that they are colored evenly. Drain the eggs and cut into quarters lengthwise. Serve with radishes and plum sauce. These eggs may be served either as a hot accompaniment to a meal or cold as an appetizer.

Tea eggs

4 American servings
4 Chinese servings

  4 eggs
  3 cups boiling water
  2 tablespoons black tea
  1 teaspoon salt
  2 cloves star anise

Place the eggs in a pan and cover with cold water. Bring to a boil over high heat. Reduce heat and simmer 5 minutes. Remove from the heat, drain the eggs and run cold water over them for several minutes. Dry the eggs and tap the shells gently on all sides to crack them evenly. Place the 3 cups boiling water in a saucepan with the tea, salt and star anise. Add the eggs, cover and simmer gently for 1½ hours. Let the eggs cool in the flavored water ½ hour. The eggs may be made in advance but do not shell them until ready to serve. Serve halved or quartered as an appetizer or as a garnish for a luncheon salad.

Steamed eggs

4 American servings
4 Chinese servings

  1 cup chicken broth
  ½ cup minced lean pork or beef
  2 scallions, minced
  2 teaspoons sherry
  ¼ teaspoon salt
  ¼ teaspoon sugar
  1 teaspoon oil
  4 eggs
  1 teaspoon oil

Heat the broth until hot but not boiling. Combine pork or beef, scallions, sherry, salt, sugar and oil in a bowl and mix until well blended. In another bowl stir the eggs just long enough to blend the yolks and whites. Add the sherry mixture and then the broth gradually, stirring gently all the time. Oil a shallow heatproof dish with the remaining oil and pour in the mixture. Steam over water that is just kept at boiling point for about 15 to 20 minutes or until of a custard-like consistency. Start testing for doneness with a toothpick after 10 minutes. When it comes out clean, the eggs are done. A little soy sauce may be sprinkled onto the eggs before serving to enhance the flavor.
Note: Minced chicken, shrimp or flaked crabmeat can be substituted for pork or beef.

Vegetables and salads

Some of the vegetables that play such an important role in Chinese cooking. Among the lesser known are bamboo, bitter melon water chestnuts, bean sprouts, bean curd and dried mushrooms.

Stir fried bean sprouts and stir fried broccoli and bean curd in oyster sauce. Tender yet crisp vegetables spread out on a bed of pure white rice grains.

Stir fried broccoli and bean curd in oyster sauce

4 American servings
8 Chinese servings

    1 pound broccoli
 ¼ cup canned bamboo shoots
    2 cakes bean curd
    2 tablespoons oyster sauce
    1 tablespoon soy sauce
 ½ cup chicken broth
    1 tablespoon cornstarch
    2 tablespoons water
    2 tablespoons oil
 ½ teaspoon salt
    2 thin slices fresh ginger root
    1 clove garlic, finely chopped

Cut off flowerets from broccoli stems. Discard tough ends and cut wide stems in half lengthwise. Then cut in 1 inch pieces diagonally. (If the stems are peeled, reduce the cooking time to 2 to 3 minutes.) In a large saucepan bring plenty of salted water to the boiling point. Add the broccoli flowerets and stems and parboil for 3 to 4 minutes. Drain and rinse broccoli under cold running water. Leave broccoli to cool completely. Cut the bamboo shoots into ¼ inch thick slices and then shred into matchsticks. Cut bean curd into ½ inch thick slices and cut slices in half crosswise. Combine oyster sauce, soy sauce and chicken broth in a saucepan and bring to simmering point over low heat. Combine the cornstarch and water. Heat 2 tablespoons oil in a wok or other pan until very hot. Add salt, ginger root and garlic. Stir fry for 1 minute until ginger root is lightly browned. Discard the ginger root. Add the drained broccoli

and stir fry for 1 minute. Add bamboo shoots, bean curd and hot chicken broth mixture. Bring to the boil again. Reduce the heat. Cover the pan and simmer for about 2 minutes or until the broccoli is tender but still quite firm. Stir in the cornstarch mixture to thicken the sauce. Serve immediately.

One of the most remarkable aspects of Chinese cooking is the approach to vegetables. They are of the utmost importance. This emphasis is due partly to the influence of the Buddist monks who established strict vegetarian rules. Small wonder this resulted in the development of extraordinary skill in preparing vegetables. To the Chinese, vegetables are not just an accompaniment to meats and other foods, but play an important role of their own. When combined with other ingredients they are at least equally as important as the meats. The main difference between the Chinese method of cooking vegetables and the Western way is that in the Chinese way, vegetables are cooked only long enough to bring out all their qualities of crispness, tenderness and brightness of color. The

vegetables are served at the peak of their flavor. This does not mean that they are served raw; even in salads, the vegetables will usually be cooked for a brief period of time. The initial preparation depends largely on how the vegetable will be used. Cutting is of the utmost importance in the preparation of vegetables. Vegetables are cut, blanched and parboiled in such a way that the final cooking can be completed at one time, even though the textures of the individual vegetables differ greatly. The soft leafy vegetables require less cooking liquid than the tougher ones. Though vegetables may be steamed, braised and even deep fried, stir frying is the favorite cooking technique. Salt and other flavorings, such as garlic or ginger root, are often added to the oil first, the vegetables are stir fried, then soy sauce and sometimes a little sugar is added. Apart from the fact that stir frying will bring out all the fine qualities that appeal to the tastebuds as well as to the eyes, vegetables prepared this way are particularly healthy because there is only a negligible loss in vitamins. After the stir frying, a liquid such as chicken broth is added and the pan is covered. To ensure their absolute freshness, vegetables should, if possible, be bought on the day they will be served. In China, bean curd is regarded as a vegetable, and its versatility is demonstrated in many of the recipes in this book.

Stir fried bean sprouts

2 American servings
4 Chinese servings

¾ pound bean sprouts
½ teaspoon salt
1 thin slice fresh ginger root, minced
½ green pepper, shredded
½ medium sized onion, shredded
3 to 4 whole scallions, shredded
2 thin slices boiled ham, shredded
2 tablespoons chicken broth combined with
½ tablespoon sherry
2 tablespoons oil

Pour boiling water over bean sprouts and let stand 20 seconds. Wash in cold running water, drain and dry on tea towels. Arrange the ingredients on a plate in the order in which they are to be cooked. Heat the oil in a wok. Add salt and ginger root and stir fry ½ minute. Add green pepper, onion and scallions and stir fry 1½ minutes. Add bean sprouts and ham and stir fry ½ minute. Add combined broth and sherry and bring to a boil. Remove from the heat and serve immediately.

Stir fried cauliflower

4 American servings
8 Chinese servings

2 cups cauliflower, flowerets only
2 tablespoons oil
2 thin slices fresh ginger root
2 scallions, minced
4 water chestnuts, thinly sliced
½ cup chicken broth
1 tablespoon sherry
1 tablespoon soy sauce
1 teaspoon oyster sauce
½ cup boiled shrimp, peeled
2 teaspoons cornstarch
1 tablespoon water

Wash cauliflower and parboil in rapidly boiling salted water for 2 to 3 minutes. Cool at once under cold running water and drain. Heat the oil in a wok or other pan, add ginger root and stir fry for 30 seconds. Add scallions and water chestnuts and stir fry for another 30 seconds. Add cauliflower, stir fry for a few seconds (just long enough to coat the vegetable with oil) and then add chicken broth, sherry, soy sauce and oyster sauce. Bring quickly to a boil and reduce heat. Add shrimp, cover and simmer for about 2 minutes. Meanwhile dissolve cornstarch in water and stir in to thicken. Serve immediately.

Celery and dried shrimp

2 American servings
4 Chinese servings

6 large stalks celery
12 dried shrimp
½ red pepper
2 cakes bean curd
3 tablespoons oil
½ cup chicken broth
3 tablespoons soy sauce
½ teaspoon sugar
⅛ teaspoon white pepper
1 teaspoon cornstarch dissolved in
1 tablespoon water

Remove leaves from celery and cut stalks in 1½ inch long pieces diagonally. Soak shrimp in hot water for 30 minutes. Drain. Remove membrane and seeds from pepper and cut into 2 inch long and ½ inch wide strips. Cut bean curd cakes into 1 inch squares. Heat the oil in a wok or other pan until quite hot, add the celery and stir fry for 45 seconds. Add the pepper and stir fry for another ½ minute over high heat. Add shrimp, bean curd, chicken broth, soy sauce, sugar and pepper. Bring to a boil over high heat. Reduce heat, cover and simmer for 15 to 20 minutes. Stir in the cornstarch to thicken and serve immediately.

Stir fried cabbage

3 American servings
6 Chinese servings

2 dried Chinese mushrooms
1 thin slice fresh ginger root, minced
½ cup chicken broth
¼ teaspoon sugar
1 tablespoon soy sauce
2 tablespoons oil
1 thin slice fresh ginger root, minced
1 pound Chinese cabbage, shredded
1 teaspoon cornstarch dissolved in
1 tablespoon water

Soak dried mushrooms in warm water for 20 minutes. Squeeze dry. Remove and discard stems and shred caps. Combine chicken broth, sugar and soy sauce in a small bowl. Heat the oil in a wok, add the ginger root and stir fry ½ minute. Add mushrooms and cabbage and stir fry 1 minute. Add the chicken broth mixture, bring to a boil and cook 2 minutes. Stir in the cornstarch mixture to thicken. Serve immediately.

Asparagus salad

4 American servings
4 Chinese servings

  1 pound asparagus
  2 tablespoons soy sauce
  1 teaspoon sugar
¼ teaspoon sesame oil
  1 teaspoon minced preserved
    red ginger (recipe page 84)

Wash asparagus, cut off tough ends and cut in a rolling cut, diagonally, into 1½ inch long pieces. Parboil tender tops for 30 seconds and the stems for 2 minutes. Drain thoroughly and place in a bowl. Mix soy sauce, sugar and sesame oil and pour over asparagus. Chill in the refrigerator 10 to 15 minutes before serving. Transfer to a serving dish, garnish with red ginger and serve.

Mushrooms in cream sauce

2 to 4 American servings
4 Chinese servings

 12 large, uniformly sized fresh
    mushrooms
  1 to 1½ tablespoons oil
½ teaspoon salt
½ cup chicken broth
½ cup heavy cream
  1 tablespoon cornstarch
  2 tablespoons water
  1 tablespoon ham garnish
    (see page 21)
  3 sprigs Chinese parsley

Remove lower part of stems from the mushrooms, but leave the caps whole. Rinse mushrooms quickly under cold running water. In a wok or other pan, heat the oil over medium heat. Add the mushrooms and salt and stir fry gently for about 2 minutes. Add chicken broth and cook for about 4 minutes. Add cream and heat to boiling point. Dissolve cornstarch in water and stir in to thicken. Transfer mushrooms to a shallow dish and cover with the sauce. Garnish with shredded ham and parsley leaves and serve hot.

Stir fried sweet and sour vegetables

2 American servings
4 Chinese servings

  1 small green pepper (or ½
    a large one)
  1 medium onion
  2 stalks celery
  2 carrots
  3 tablespoons vinegar
  2 tablespoons sugar
  1 tablespoon sherry
  2 tablespoons chicken broth
    or water
  2 tablespoons oil
  1 clove garlic, crushed
  2 thin slices fresh ginger root,
    minced
½ cup shredded canned
    bamboo shoots
¼ teaspoon white pepper
  1 tablespoon cornstarch
    dissolved in
  2 tablespoons water

Remove membrane and seeds from pepper and cut into 2 inch long diamond shapes. Peel the onion, halve lengthwise and cut each half into ½ inch wide strips lengthwise. Cut celery in 2 inch pieces diagonally. Cut carrots in a rolling cut, diagonally, into 1½ inch pieces. Heat vinegar. Remove from heat and add sugar, sherry and broth. Cover to keep warm. Heat oil in a wok or other pan until quite hot. Add garlic, ginger root and carrots and stir fry for 1 minute. Add all other ingredients and stir fry over high heat for about 2 minutes. Add vinegar mixture and stir fry for another 2 minutes. Stir in cornstarch mixture to thicken and serve.

Radish and cucumber salad

4 to 6 American servings
4 to 6 Chinese servings

  About 16 to 20 radishes
½ cucumber
  1 tablespoon salt
  4 tablespoons vinegar
  2 teaspoons sugar
½ teaspoon salt
  2 tablespoons soy sauce
¼ teaspoon sesame oil

Cut radishes into radish roses as described in recipe on page 21 (shredded lettuce and radish garnishes). Remove ends of the cucumber and then quarter lengthwise. Scoop out seedy center to leave about ½ to ¾ inch thickness. Cut into 2 inch long pieces and then into slices ⅛ inch thick. Sprinkle radishes and cucumber with salt and leave for about 10 minutes. Rinse under cold running water. Drain thoroughly. Meanwhile, bring vinegar to a boil in a small enamelled saucepan. Stir in sugar and salt until dissolved. Cool the liquid and stir in soy sauce and sesame oil. Pour over radishes and cucumber and place in the refrigerator for about ½ hour. Pour off excess liquid and carefully spread cucumber into a fanlike design on a serving plate. Decorate the plate with radish roses. This salad may be served as a side dish or with appetizers.

Sub gum vegetables: 10 different colors, tastes and textures assembled in one dish.

Sub gum vegetables

4 to 6 American servings
4 to 6 Chinese servings

  1 *sweet red or green pepper*
  1 *medium onion*
  2 *carrots*
  ½ *cup bamboo shoots*
  ½ *cup water chestnuts*
  2 *stalks celery*
  ½ *cup fresh mushrooms*
  2 *dried Chinese mushrooms*
  4 *tablespoons oil*
  ½ *teaspoon salt*
  ¾ *cup bean sprouts*
  4 *tablespoons water*
  2 *tablespoons soy sauce*
  1 *tablespoon sherry*
  ½ *teaspoon sugar*
  1 *tablespoon cornstarch*
  2 *tablespoons water*
  ½ *teaspoon sesame oil*

Remove seeds and membranes from pepper and cut into 2 inch long diamond shapes. Peel the onion, halve lengthwise and cut each half in ½ inch wide strips lengthwise. Cut the carrots diagonally, in a rolling cut, into 1½ inch pieces. Cut the bamboo shoots in ⅛ inch thick slices and halve them if they are large pieces. Cut water chestnuts in ½ inch thick slices crosswise. Cut celery in 2 inch pieces diagonally. Cut fresh mushrooms in half if small or in thick slices if large mushrooms are used. Soak Chinese mushrooms in hot water for about 20 minutes. Cut off the stems and cut caps in ½ inch wide strips. Heat 2 tablespoons oil in a large wok or other pan until quite hot. Add half of the salt and stir fry for 30 seconds. Add pepper and

onion and stir fry for 1 minute. Remove from the pan. Add another tablespoon of oil, heat, add celery and both kinds of mushrooms and stir fry for 1 minute. Add bean sprouts and stir fry for another ½ minute. Remove from the pan and add another tablespoon oil. Add carrots and bamboo shoots and stir fry for 1½ minutes. Add water chestnuts and stir fry for another 1 minute. Sprinkle with remaining salt, add water, soy sauce, sherry and sugar and bring quickly to the boil. Add all the vegetables and, when boiling again, cover, reduce heat a little and cook for 1½ to 2 minutes. Stir in cornstarch dissolved in the water and sesame oil and serve.

Stuffed green peppers

4 American servings
8 Chinese servings

1½ *cups minced lean pork*
  1 *tablespoon minced bamboo shoots*
  4 *medium sized fresh mushrooms, minced*
  1 *scallion, minced*
  2 *thin slices fresh ginger root, minced*
  2 *tablespoons soy sauce*
  2 *tablespoons sherry*
  ½ *teaspoon sugar*
  ⅛ *teaspoon pepper*
  1 *teaspoon cornstarch*
  4 *green peppers, halved and seeded*
  2 *tablespoons oil*
  ½ *cup chicken broth*
  2 *tablespoons soy sauce*
  1 *tomato, peeled, seeded and finely chopped*
  1 *tablespoon cornstarch dissolved in*
  2 *tablespoons water*
  4 *onion brushes (recipe page 20)*

Mix first 10 ingredients. Fill pepper with this mixture. Heat the oil in a wok until very hot. Carefully place pepper halves in the wok, stuffing side down. Fry 1½ to 2 minutes over medium heat or until browned. Add broth, soy sauce and tomato and bring to a boil. Reduce heat, cover and simmer 7 minutes. Turn peppers over, cover and cook 5 more minutes. Transfer the peppers to a serving dish. Thicken sauce with cornstarch mixture. Pour over peppers and garnish with onion brushes.

Stuffed bean curd

6 American servings
6 Chinese servings

  6 cakes bean curd
*½ to ¾ pound lean pork,
     minced*
  2 scallions, minced
  *2 water chestnuts, minced
     (optional)*
½ tablespoon soy sauce
  1 tablespoon sherry
  1 egg yolk
1½ tablespoons oil
¼ teaspoon salt
  1 thin slice fresh ginger root
  1 clove garlic
  *1 cup celery cabbage or other
     seasonal green vegetable,
     cut into 1½ inch diamonds*
¾ cup chicken broth
  2 tablespoons soy sauce
  1 tablespoon sherry
  1 tablespoon cornstarch
  2 tablespoons water

Cut the bean curd cakes in half.
Make a pocket in each half
to contain the filling. Take care
not to break the bean curd.
In a bowl, mix together the
pork, scallions and water
chestnuts. Add soy sauce,
sherry and egg yolk and mix
well. Stuff the bean curd
carefully with this mixture.
Place the bean curd on a large,
shallow heat proof dish and
steam for about 25 minutes.
Meanwhile, about 5 minutes
before the steaming is completed,
heat the oil in a wok or a
skillet. Stir in the salt and add
the ginger and garlic clove.
Stir fry for 1 minute until
golden brown. Discard the
ginger and garlic. Increase the
heat, add the celery cabbage
and stir fry for 1 minute. Add
chicken broth, soy sauce and
sherry. Reduce the heat, cover
and continue cooking for 1½
minutes. Dissolve the cornstarch
in water and stir into the
cabbage. Cook 30 seconds until
thickened. Remove steaming
dish. Add cabbage and sauce
and serve immediately.

Rice dishes

Rice and noodles are the staple food of the Chinese people. Rice is grown and eaten primarily in the Southern part of China where it is important not only for its taste but because it is often the only barrier against starvation. But even apart from the basic necessity of eating rice, to the Chinese, the pure white grains and bland taste seem to be the perfect accompaniment to all other foods. When sampling all the myriad taste elements of a Chinese meal, a spoonful of rice taken with the other food as well as in between, brings a neutral element into play so that every new morsel can unfold all its full flavor and character.

Long grain rice is suitable for most dishes. When properly cooked, it absorbs a great deal of water and will be dry and fluffy. Short grain rice, because it does not absorb as much water as the long grain variety, will generally be softer and more moist and the grains will tend to stick to one another. The so called instant rice is not suitable for Chinese cooking; it has less taste and is less nutritious. Rice is either boiled or steamed, though even in boiling there is actually a steaming process going on in the pan for most of the time. It is very important to wash the rice well to get ride of the excess starch which otherwise would make the rice too sticky. After it has been boiled or steamed, left over rice can be fried. It should be completely cooled before it is fried. Sometimes rice is not cooked alone, but may be topped with other foods, the flavors of which are allowed to permeate the rice.

Fried rice I

4 American servings
4 Chinese servings

  3 cups cold cooked rice
  3 eggs
¼ teaspoon salt
½ tablespoon water
  2 tablespoons oil
  2 scallions, cut into ½ inch pieces
  2 tablespoons soy sauce

Separate the grains of rice with chopsticks or a fork. Lightly beat the eggs, salt and water. Heat the oil in a wok. Add the scallions and stir fry ½ minute. Add the rice and stir fry until heated through and each grain is coated with oil. Pour in the egg mixture and continue stirring until the egg is nearly set. Add soy sauce and stir until well combined. Serve. immediately.

Fried rice II

4 American servings
4 Chinese servings

  3 cups cold cooked rice
  2 eggs
¼ teaspoon salt
½ tablespoon sherry
  2 tablespoons oil
  4 scallions, cut into ½ inch pieces
½ cup diced roast pork (recipe page 33)
½ cup diced cooked smoked ham
½ cup cooked peas
  2 tablespoons chicken broth
  1 tablespoon soy sauce

Separate the grains of rice with chopsticks or a fork. Lightly beat the eggs, salt and sherry. Heat the oil in a wok. Add the scallions, roast pork and ham and stir fry ½ minute. Add the rice and stir fry until heated through and each grain is coated with oil. Add the peas and pour in the egg mixture. Continue stirring until the egg is nearly set. Add chicken broth and soy sauce and stir until well combined. Serve immediately.

Eight jewel fried rice

6 American servings
6 Chinese servings

    4 cups cold cooked rice
    4 eggs
    ½ teaspoon salt
    1 tablespoon water
    3½ tablespoons oil
    2 scallions
    4 large shrimp
    ½ cup diced lean pork
    ½ cup diced cooked boiled ham
      or uncooked smoked ham
    ½ cup diced chicken breast
    4 fresh mushrooms, finely
      chopped
    3 water chestnuts, sliced
      thinly
    ½ cup cooked peas
    ¼ teaspoon salt
    1 tablespoon soy sauce
    2 to 3 tablespoons chicken
      broth

Loosen the cold rice with chopsticks or your fingers to separate it into individual grains. Combine the eggs, salt and water in a small bowl and beat lightly. Scramble the eggs in 1 tablespoon oil until just set. Remove the eggs from the pan. Cut the scallions into pieces ½ inch long. Shell, devein and chop the shrimp into small pieces. Heat the remaining oil in a wok or a skillet. Add scallions and stir fry for 30 seconds. Add pork and stir fry for about 2 minutes or until it has lost any trace of pink. Add ham, chicken breast and mushrooms and stir fry for 1 minute. Add shrimp and water chestnuts and stir fry for another 1 minute. Add rice and stir fry for 1 minute.

Add peas, salt, soy sauce and chicken broth. Add scrambled eggs to pan. Stir fry gently to allow rice to heat through. Serve hot.

Sizzling rice

4 American servings
4 Chinese servings

This dish, sometimes called singing rice or crackling rice, is made with the crusts of rice which remain sticking to the pan when cooking rice. As this is normally only 1 or 2 tablespoons, you have to "collect" these crusts from several batches of cooked rice until you have the cup and a half you need for this recipe. Rice crusts may be reserved in any airtight capped container in the refrigerator for several weeks.

    1½ cups rice crusts
    1 pound shrimp
    1½ tablespoons sherry
    ¼ teaspoon salt
    1 tablespoon cornstarch
    2 tablespoons oil or lard
    ¾ cup chicken broth
    ¼ teaspoon salt
    1 tablespoon sugar
    4 tablespoons tomato purée
      or catsup
    ½ tablespoon sherry
    1 tablespoon cornstarch
    2 tablespoons water
      Oil for deep frying

Break the rice crusts into bite size pieces and dry on a baking sheet in a 300 degree oven for 10 minutes or until completely dry. Shell the shrimp and take out the black vein. Combine sherry, salt and cornstarch and mix with the shrimp. Leave for 20 minutes. Heat the oil or lard in a wok or other pan. Add the shrimp and stir fry for about 1 minute or until pink but not completely done. Remove shrimp from pan and keep warm. Combine chicken broth, salt, sugar, tomato purée or catsup and sherry in a saucepan and bring to a boil. Mix cornstarch and water and stir into the sauce to thicken. Add shrimp, reduce heat a little and simmer for 2 minutes or until heated through. Heat the oil for deep frying, when oil is quite hot, add rice crusts and deep fry for about 1 minute or until floating and golden brown. Remove rice from pan with a skimmer, drain quickly and place on a hot serving dish. Bring rice and shrimp sauce to the table. Pour the sauce over the hot rice and you will hear the rice sizzle and sing with happiness.

Congee for break fast, simple rice and sausages for lunch and Eight jewel fried rice (recipe page 75, 1st column) for dinner. Rice is appreciated in its dominant role.

Cooked rice and and sausages

4 American servings
4 Chinese servings

  1 cup raw rice
1½ to 1¾ cups water
  2 to 3 Chinese sausages, cut
     into ¼ inch diagonal slices
     Parsley sprigs

Cook the rice as described in rice cooking I (recipe page 18). After most of the water has been absorbed by the rice, place the sausage slices on top of the rice. Cover the pan and continue cooking as directed. Place the sausage and rice in a serving bowl and garnish with parsley sprigs.

Note: The sausage may be sprinkled with 1 tablespoon sherry before adding to the rice. Dried Chinese mushroom caps which have been soaked in warm water for 20 minutes and shredded may also be added with the mushrooms.

Roast duck congee

3 American servings
5 Chinese servings

  ½ cup uncooked rice
  6 cups water
  2 small dried scallops or
     substitute 2 tablespoons
     dried shrimp or 1½
     teaspoons salt
  1 small piece tangerine peel
  1 cup roast duck, wings, legs,
     etc., cut into bite size
     pieces (see page 90)
  ½ tablespoon sherry
  1 tablespoon scallion, green
     part only, cut into small rings

Place the rice and water in a pan. Add scallops, shrimp or salt and tangerine peel. Bring to a boil over high heat. Reduce heat, cover and simmer for about 45 minutes. Add roast duck and sherry. Cover and simmer for at least 1 hour, stirring occasionally and adding some water if the congee becomes too thick. Remove tangerine peel and dried scallops or dried shrimp, if desired. Top with scallions and serve.

Noodle dishes

Noodles with a very special meat sauce and soft fried noodles with pork and shrimp (recipe page 78, 1st column). The first resembles the Italian spaghetti and Bolognese sauce.

Noodles and meat sauce

Noodles are the food of the North. They are made mainly from grains but sometimes also from seaweed or the starch of mung peas. Noodles are almost always made in thin threads, but there is considerable variety in texture, thickness and width. They can be boiled, steamed, soft fried, deep fried and used in soups.

4 American servings
6 Chinese servings

  5 scallions
½ cucumber
  1 clove garlic
  1 thin slice fresh ginger root
¼ cup bamboo shoots (optional)
  3 fresh mushrooms
  2 tablespoons Chinese brown bean sauce (or Japanese akamiso)
½ pound lean pork
  1 pound egg noodles
  1 tablespoon oil
  2 tablespoons oil
½ teaspoon salt
½ teaspoon sugar
½ tablespoon sherry

¼ cup beef broth
  1 tablespoon soy sauce or hoisin sauce

Cut 2 scallions into 2-inch long pieces, then shred lengthwise. Mince remaining scallions. Peel cucumber, cut in ¼-inch thick slices and then shred. Mince garlic and ginger root finely. Dice bamboo shoots and mushrooms finely. Rub brown bean sauce through a sieve. Mince the pork. Cook noodles as described on page 19, rinse under cold water, drain and mix with 1 tablespoon oil. Reheat and keep warm.

Heat 2 tablespoons oil in a wok or other pan. Add salt, garlic and ginger root and stir fry for 30 seconds. Add minced green onions and stir fry for another ½ minute. Then add pork and stir fry for about 1 to 1½ minutes or until it has lost any trace of pink. Add bamboo shoots and mushrooms and stir fry for another ½ minute. Stir in brown bean sauce, sugar, sherry, and soy sauce or hoisin sauce. Reduce heat, cover and simmer for about 4 minutes. Put noodles in hot bowl and pour over the sauce. Garnish with cucumber and scallions and serve immediately.

Soft fried noodles, pork and shrimp

4 American servings
8 Chinese servings

  1 *recipe soft fried noodles*
     (recipe page 79)
½ *pound lean pork*
½ *pound shrimp*
  1 *stalk celery, cut diagonally*
     in ¾ inch pieces
  3 *tablespoons oil*
¼ *teaspoon salt*
  1 *tablespoon soy sauce*
  1 *tablespoon sherry*
  1 *clove garlic, crushed*
  1 *slice fresh ginger root,*
     minced
½ *red pepper, seeded and cut*
     into ½ inch long pieces
1½ *tablespoons chicken broth*
     or water
  1 *recipe egg-garnish*
     (recipe page 21)
  6 *onion brushes (recipe*
     page 20)

Prepare soft fried noodles as described in previous recipe. Cut pork in strips 1½ inches long, ½ inch wide and ⅛ inch thick. Shell shrimp and take out the black vein. Blanch the celery in boiling water for 3 minutes. Rinse under cold running water and drain. Heat 2 tablespoons oil in a wok or other pan. Add salt and stir fry for about 30 seconds. Add pork and stir fry for about 2 minutes or until it has lost any trace of pink. Add shrimp and stir fry for about 1 minute. Add soy sauce and sherry and stir fry for another 30 seconds. Remove pork and shrimp mixture from pan. Add remaining oil and heat. Add garlic and ginger root and stir

fry for 30 seconds. Discard garlic, add celery and red pepper and stir fry for about 1½ minutes. Add broth and stir fry for another minute. Return pork and shrimp to the pan and heat through briefly. Add soft fried noodles and toss to mix. Transfer to a serving dish, garnish with egg-garnish and onion brushes and serve.

Mixed tossed noodles

4 American servings
6 Chinese servings

  1 *pound egg noodles*
  1 *tablespoon oil*
  4 *scallions*
  2 *dried Chinese mushrooms*
½ *cup cooked chicken*
½ *cup roast pork*
  3 *tablespoons oil*
  1 *clove garlic, crushed*
  1 *thin slice fresh ginger*
     root, minced
½ *cup bamboo shoots, shredded*
½ *cup bean sprouts*
½ *cup chicken broth*
  3 *tablespoons soy sauce*
  1 *tablespoon sherry*
½ *teaspoon sugar*
  1 *tablespoon cornstarch*
  2 *tablespoons water*
  2 *tablespoons ham garnish*
     (recipe page 21)

Cook the noodles as described on page 19. Drain noodles and rinse under cold running water. Toss with 1 tablespoon oil. Cut scallions into pieces ½ inch long. Soak dried mushrooms in hot water for 20 minutes. Squeeze mushrooms dry. Discard stems and cut caps into strips 1 inch long and ¼ inch wide. Cut chicken into slices ¼ inch thick. Cook pork as described on page 33. Cut pork into ¼ inch thick slices. Heat the oil in a wok or large skillet. Add garlic and ginger and stir fry for 30 seconds. Add scallions and stir fry for 30 seconds. Add bamboo shoots and mushrooms and stir fry for 1½ minutes. Add chicken and pork and stir fry for 1 minute. Add bean

sprouts and stir fry for 20 seconds. Add chicken broth, soy sauce, sherry and sugar. Bring to a boil over high heat. Combine cornstarch and water and add to thicken sauce. Immerse noodles in boiling water for 2 minutes until very hot. Drain noodles and place in a serving dish. Add stir fried mixture and toss gently. Serve immediately.

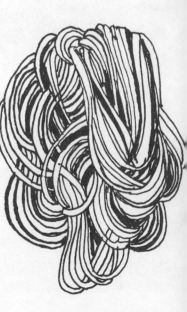

Plain soft fried noodles

6 *American servings*
6 *Chinese servings*

  1 *pound egg noodles*
  1 *tablespoon oil*
  2 *scallions*
  3 *tablespoons oil*
  ½ *teaspoon salt*
  1 *teaspoon soy sauce*

Cook noodles as described in recipe on page 19. Drain, rinse under cold running water and mix with 1 tablespoon oil. Cut scallions in ½ inch long pieces. Heat the oil in a wok or other pan until quite hot. Add scallions and stir fry for 30 seconds. Add noodles and stir fry for 2 minutes, separating the noodles with chopsticks. Add salt and soy sauce and stir fry for another ½ to 1 minute or until completely heated through and lightly browned. Serve plain or combine with a stir fried mixture as indicated in other recipes.

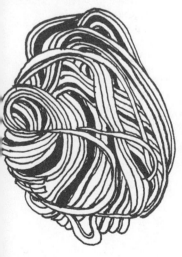

Soft fried rice noodles

4 *American servings*
8 *Chinese servings*

  1 *pound rice noodles*
  1 *tablespoon oil*
  ¼ *cup dried shrimp (optional)*
  2 *to 3 dried Chinese mushrooms*
  ½ *pound lean pork*
  ¼ *cup preserved tea melon or preserved sweet cucumber*
  4 *tablespoons oil*
  3 *scallions, cut into ½ inch pieces*
  1 *tablespoon soy sauce*
  ¼ *cup shredded bamboo shoots*
  4 *fresh mushrooms, thinly sliced*
  ¼ *cup sliced water chestnuts*
  1 *tablespoon chicken broth or water*

Parboil rice noodles for 7 to 8 minutes. Drain, rinse under cold running water and mix with 1 tablespoon oil. Meanwhile, soak dried shrimp and dried mushrooms separately in warm water for about 30 minutes. Drain shrimp and squeeze mushrooms dry. Remove mushroom stems and shred caps. Cut the pork into pieces 1 inch long, ¾ inch wide and ½ inch thick. Drain tea melon and cut into ½ to ¾ inch long pieces. Heat 2 tablespoons oil in a wok or other pan. Add scallions and stir fry for about 30 seconds. Add pork and stir fry for about 2 minutes or until it has lost any trace of pink. Add dried shrimp and stir fry for another 30 seconds. Add soy sauce, bamboo shoots, mushrooms, dried mushrooms and water chestnuts and stir fry for 1½ minutes. Add broth and tea melon and stir fry for another ½ minute. Remove from pan and keep warm. Add remaining oil to the pan and heat until very hot. Add noodles and stir fry for 1 to 1½ minutes or until heated through and very lightly browned. Return meats and vegetables to the wok and toss to mix. Serve immediately.

Noodles in soup I

4 *American servings*
4 *Chinese servings*

  3 *cups chicken broth*
  ¼ *cup shredded Chinese cabbage or spinach*
  ½ *cup shredded roast pork (recipe page 33)*
  1 *scallion, cut in 1 inch pieces*
  1 *teaspoon soy sauce*
  ¼ *pound egg noodles, cooked (recipe page 19)*
  4 *sprigs fresh parsley*

Bring broth to the simmer. Add cabbage and simmer 3 minutes. Add pork and scallion and simmer 1 minute. Stir in soy sauce. Place noodles in individual soup bowls. With a slotted spoon, place some of the pork and vegetables in each bowl. Pour the broth into the bowls, garnish with parsley and serve.

Noodles in soup, served in a Nga Po casserole dish and soft fried rice noodles which has tea melon as one of its interesting ingredients, (page 79).

Noodles in soup II

4 American servings
4 Chinese servings

¼ pound egg noodles
1 dried Chinese mushroom
2 ounces lean pork (butt or shoulder)
½ tablespoon sherry
¼ teaspoon salt
1 teaspoon cornstarch
1½ tablespoons oil
1 thin slice fresh ginger root, minced
2 fresh mushrooms, thinly sliced
1 tablespoon soy sauce
3 cups boiling chicken broth
4 onion brushes (recipe page 20)

Parboil noodles as directed in recipe on page 19 and keep warm. Soak dried mushroom in warm water for about 20 minutes. Squeeze dry, remove stem and shred cap. Cut pork into ⅛ to ¼ inch thick slices across the grain. Mix sherry, salt and cornstarch. Add pork and toss to coat. Heat the oil in a wok or frying pan. Add the ginger root and stir fry for 30 seconds. Add the pork and stir fry for about 1½ minutes. Add fresh and dried mushrooms and stir fry for another half minute. Add soy sauce to the boiling broth. Place the noodles in individual bowls and pour over the broth. Top with stir fried pork and mushrooms, garnish each serving with an onion brush and serve.

Sauces

*These are the ingredients that
keep a Master sauce alive.*

The Chinese have two main
categories of sauces. A number of
sauces are incorporated into the
dish and have already been mixed
with the other ingredients by the
cook. The other group of sauces
are served on the table as dipping
sauces.

The first category includes the
famous sweet-sour sauces which
are frequently served with deep
fried foods. The small amount of
sauce which always accompanies
stir fried dishes and the meat
sauce served on the noodles are
also considered part of the first
category.

Though there are quite a few of
these sauces in the Chinese
repertoire, they are far
outnumbered by the sauces and
dips used on the table. The last
group also includes the dry mixes
like salt and pepper mix (see
recipe on page 83) and other
condiments, pickles and dressings
either packaged or homemade.
Marinades are also widely used
in Chinese cooking to flavor and
tenderize the food before it is
actually cooked. The Master
Sauce is perhaps the most
interesting of all the sauces, a full
description of which can be found
on page 22.

Sweet sour sauce I

½ cup sugar
½ cup vinegar
2 tablespoons soy sauce
2 tablespoons sherry
3 tablespoons tomato sauce
    or tomato catsup
2 tablespoons cornstarch
    dissolved in
½ cup water or pineapple juice

Place the sugar, vinegar, soy
sauce, sherry and tomato sauce
in a heavy saucepan. Bring to a
boil and add the cornstarch
mixture, stirring constantly
until the sauce is thickened.
Use as directed in recipes.

Sweet sour sauce II

½ cup sugar
½ cup vinegar
4 to 5 tablespoons light
soy sauce
1 tablespoon dark soy
sauce (optional)
2 tablespoons sherry
1½ tablespoons cornstarch
dissolved in
½ cup water

Place sugar, vinegar, light soy sauce, dark soy sauce and sherry in a heavy saucepan. Bring to a boil and stir in the cornstarch mixture to thicken. Use as directed in recipes.

Sweet sour sauce III

¼ inch thick slice fresh ginger
root, chopped
½ cup sugar
½ cup vinegar
6 tablespoons water or
pineapple juice
1 tablespoon sherry
1½ tablespoons cornstarch
dissolved in
4 tablespoons water

Using a garlic press, squeeze the ginger juice into a heavy saucepan. Add the sugar, vinegar, water or pineapple juice and sherry. Bring the sauce to a boil and stir in the cornstarch mixture to thicken. Use as directed in recipes.

Sauce for foo young eggs

¾ cup chicken broth
½ teaspoon salt
1 tablespoon soy sauce
2 teaspoons sherry
3 teaspoons tomato catsup
¼ teaspoon sugar
2 teaspoons cornstarch
1½ tablespoons water

Bring chicken broth to boiling point. Add salt, soy sauce, sherry, catsup and sugar. Stir to blend. Dissolve cornstarch in water and stir to thicken.
Note: Oyster sauce may be substituted for tomato catsup in this recipe.

Master sauce

This is a sauce which can go on for ever and ever and, like a good wine, improves with age. However, it is worth the trouble only if you like red simmered dishes and intend to make them regularly. To make this sauce, prepare any of the red simmered dishes in this book. Eat the meat and reserve the sauce. Strain it through a layer of cheesecloth. Skim off the fat, pour it into a jar and refrigerate. The next time you prepare a red simmered dish, cook the meat in this sauce instead of using the liquid ingredients mentioned in the specific recipe. Not only will the meat taste better, but the sauce will improve with the addition of the new meat juices. In each subsequent preparation, the meat or chicken as well as the sauce will become richer in taste and flavor, especially when you add some soy sauce, sherry, sugar, scallion, ginger root and salt every third time you use the sauce. After using the sauce 6 or 8 times, you may add a little star anise, cinnamon or a pinch of five spice powder. A few tablespoons of fresh meat broth may be added from time to time to rejuvenate the sauce. If the sauce has not been used for a week, it is necessary to bring it to a boil again. Cool it to room temperature and refrigerate. This will keep the sauce from becoming sour. The sauce may very well outlive you and be inherited by your children as it was and still is in some Chinese families!

Oyster sauce

If bottled oyster sauce is not available, a fair substitute can be made following this recipe. Do not use smoked oysters or any other flavored preparation.

1 (8 ounce) can oysters
1 tablespoon water
1 teaspoon salt
Soy sauce
½ tablespoon dark soy sauce

Drain the oysters and reserve the liquid. Mince the oysters and place them in a saucepan. Add water and reserved oyster liquid and bring to a boil over low heat. Reduce heat, cover and simmer for about 10 minutes. Remove from the heat, add salt and let cool completely. Force the mixture through a fine sieve into a heavy saucepan and discard the minced oysters. Measure the liquid, adding 2 tablespoons soy sauce to each ½ cup of oyster liquid. Add the dark soy sauce and bring to a boil. Reduce heat and simmer over low heat for about 7 minutes. Let cool to room temperature and pour into a clear jar. Seal and store in the refrigerator. This sauce can be kept for several weeks.

Plum sauce

1 cup fresh plums, pitted and finely chopped
¼ cup dried apricots, soaked in warm water 1 hour and finely chopped
⅛ teaspoon cayenne pepper
1 teaspoon salt
1 to 2 tablespoons water
½ to ¾ cup sugar
½ cup vinegar

Place the plums and apricots in a heavy saucepan. Add cayenne pepper, salt and about 1 tablespoon water. Bring to a boil over low heat and simmer 15 minutes. Add a little more water if the mixture becomes too dry. Stir in sugar and vinegar and simmer 20 to 30 minutes or until the sauce reaches a chutney-like consistency. Place the sauce in a covered jar and refrigerate when cool. The sauce will keep several months.

Pepper and salt mix

3 tablespoons salt
2 tablespoons Szechuan peppercorns or crushed black peppercorns

Heat a heavy skillet until very hot. Place salt and peppercorns in the skillet. Reduce the heat and stir the mixture 5 to 6 minutes or until the salt is light brown. Remove from the pan and crush the peppercorns in a mortar. Sift the mixture through a sieve. Store the pepper and salt mix in a tightly covered jar.

Dip sauces

Soy-oil dip sauce

2 tablespoons oil
1 teaspoon finely minced scallions, white part only
½ teaspoon ginger root, finely minced
4 tablespoons soy sauce

Heat the oil in a small saucepan until hot. Add scallions and ginger root. Stir fry 20 to 30 seconds. Add soy sauce. Remove from heat and stir to mix well. Serve with white cooked chicken.

Sherry-soy dip sauce

2 tablespoons sherry
2 tablespoons soy sauce
¼ teaspoon sugar

Stir the above ingredients together until the sugar has dissolved. Serve as a dip for white cooked or deep fried chicken.

Oyster sauce (recipe page 83, 1st column), preserved red ginger and plum sauce can also easily be made at home, (recipe page 83, 2nd column).

Preserved red ginger

½ pound fresh ginger root
1 tablespoon salt
1½ to 2 cups vinegar
8 to 10 tablespoons sugar
½ teaspoon red food coloring

Scrape the thin outer skin from the ginger root. Cut it into ⅛ inch thick slices and then into thin strips about 1½ inches long. Sprinkle with salt and let stand 2 hours. Rinse thoroughly and drain. Heat the vinegar in a heavy saucepan and stir in the sugar until dissolved. Add ginger root, cover and simmer gently for about 10 minutes. Remove from the heat, add food coloring and stir. Let cool completely. Transfer to a glass jar, cap and refrigerate. Preserved red ginger will keep for at least 1 year or longer. Use for decoration and as described in recipe for asparagus salad (page 71).

Desserts

There are only a few Chinese desserts but this simple Almond cookie and the scooped out and decorated watermelon filled with lychees and other fruits, make up for the absence of a wide choice.

Watermelon and lychees

8 American servings
12 Chinese servings

> 1 watermelon
> 1 (16 ounce) can lychees in syrup
> 1 (16 ounce) can pitted cherries, Mandarin oranges or other fruit (or a combination of several), drained

Cut away the top of the watermelon about ¼ of the way down to form a boat. Scoop out the fruit with a melon ball scoop, making neat round balls. Combine the watermelon balls, lychees with their syrup and cherries. Scoop out the ridges in the watermelon boat, making sure to leave a 1 inch thickness of rind. The edges of the rind may be decorated with a vegetable notcher. Place the combined fruits in the watermelon boat and chill 1 hour before serving.

It is often a great disappointment for people to discover that the Chinese have only a very limited range of desserts and sweets. And out of this limited range, most desserts are not even served with family meals, but reserved for banquets and formal dinners. Even in the bakery section there are only very few sweet foods, and the cakes are steamed rather than baked in the oven. But even though there are so few desserts, the lack is one of quantity rather than quality. The recipes in this section are all fine creations which can stand comparison with desserts from all over the world. You only need to look at a beautiful fruit filled watermelon bowl (page 85) to see that this is true.

Almond cookies

30 to 40 cookies

1 cup sugar
1 cup lard
1 egg
2 teaspoons almond extract
3 cups all purpose flour
1½ teaspoons baking powder
¼ teaspoon salt
¾ cup blanched, slivered almonds
  Whole blanched almonds for decoration

Cream the sugar and lard together until light and fluffy. Beat in the egg and almond extract. Sift together the flour, baking powder and salt. Add 1 cup of the flour mixture and all of the slivered almonds and combine thoroughly. Add the rest of the flour, ½ cup at a time. (You may have to knead in the last bit.) Knead the dough until it is firm and pliable. Roll it out to a ¼ to ½ inch thickness on a floured board. Cut the cookies with a 1½ to 2 inch round cookie cutter. Transfer to a lightly oiled cookie sheet. Place a whole blanched almond in the center of each cookie. Bake in a preheated 350° oven for 20 minutes or until light brown. Cool on wire racks.

Almond float

6 American servings
6 Chinese servings

For the gelatin:
  1 cup blanched slivered almonds, finely ground
  3 cups water
  ¼ cup sugar
  1½ packages unflavored gelatin

For the fruit:
  3 cups water
  ¾ cup sugar
  2 cups drained canned Mandarin oranges, pitted cherries, lychees or a combination of all 3

Place the almonds, 2½ cups water and ¼ cup sugar in a saucepan. Bring to a boil stirring constantly. Reduce heat and simmer, stirring occasionally, for 15 minutes. Meanwhile, sprinkle gelatin over ½ cup cold water. Strain the almond mixture pressing as much liquid as possible out of the almonds. Add the gelatin to the hot liquid, stirring to dissolve. Pour into an 8 × 8 × 2 inch pan and refrigerate until set. Bring the remaining 3 cups water to a boil. Add the sugar and stir until dissolved. Cool the liquid to room temperature, add the fruit and chill. When ready to serve, cut the almond gelatin into diamond shapes. Place the fruit and syrup in a serving bowl. "Float" the diamonds in the syrup and serve.

Steamed sponge cake

4 eggs, separated
1 cup sugar
½ teaspoon vanilla extract
1 cup flour
½ teaspoon baking powder

Beat the egg whites until stiff. Beat the egg yolks separately with the sugar and vanilla extract until creamy. Fold in egg whites. Sift flour and baking powder together and stir into egg mixture until well blended. Oil a square 8 inch cake pan very lightly and pour in the batter. Place in a steamer and steam for about 25 minutes. Test with a tooth pick. If it comes out clean, the cake is done. Remove from pan and let cool for 10 minutes. Invert cake onto a platter and cut into 2 inch squares. May be served hot or cold.

4 to 6 American servings
4 to 6 Chinese servings

4 firm apples
1 egg
1 egg white
2 tablespoons flour
2 tablespoons cornstarch
  Oil for deep frying
¼ cup oil
¼ cup sugar
¼ cup honey
1½ tablespoons white sesame seeds (optional)
1 bowl of ice water

Peel and core the apples and cut each apple in 6 to 8 wedges. Beat egg and egg white until well blended and beat in the flour and cornstarch. Heat the oil for deep frying until hot. Dip apple wedges in the batter and deep fry until golden. Remove and drain on paper towels. In a saucepan, heat ¼ cup oil, add the sugar and heat, stirring constantly, until the sugar has dissolved. Stir in the honey. Coat apple fritters with the syrup. Transfer fritters and syrup to a bowl and sprinkle with sesame seeds. Bring to the table while still piping hot. Let each guest dip the apple fritters into the ice water. This will cause the syrup coating to harden so that the fritters will be crisp and crackling on the outside.

Peking dust

6 *American servings*
8 *Chinese servings*

   2 *pounds chestnuts or 1
    (1 pound) can unsweetened
    chestnut purée*
¼ *cup sugar*
   2 *cups heavy cream*
   3 *tablespoons powdered sugar*
   1 *teaspoon vanilla extract*
   1 *tablespoon brown sugar,
    sifted*
¼ *cup water*
½ *cup sugar*
¼ *cup canned Mandarin
    oranges*
¼ *cup pitted cherries or
    blanched almonds*

Score chestnuts crosswise on
their flat side. Place them on
a baking sheet and heat them
in a 400° oven for about
15 minutes or until slightly
opened. Skin them when they
are cool enough to handle.
Place the chestnuts in a pan
and cover with water. Bring to
a boil and cook for about 35
minutes or until just tender.
Force the chestnuts through a
sieve and combine with the
¼ cup sugar. If canned
chestnut purée is used, simply
combine it with the sugar.
Whip the cream until slightly
thickened. Beat in the powdered
sugar and vanilla and continue
beating until very stiff. Divide
the cream into 2 equal portions.
Fold the brown sugar and the
chestnut purée into 1 portion
of the cream until well blended.
Lightly oil a bowl just large
enough to hold the chestnut
mixture. Place it in the bowl
and press down firmly. Invert
the chestnut cream onto a
plate and top with the remaining
cream. Bring the water to a
boil. Add the sugar and boil
until syrupy. Dip the fruits
and nuts, if used, into the
syrup. Let them cool and
harden on a greased surface.
Decorate the Peking Dust with
the glacéed fruits in a beautiful
pattern.

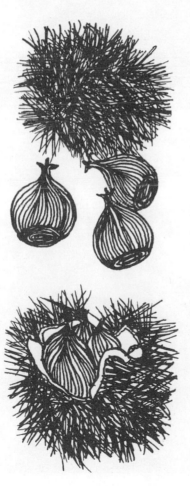

Eight precious pudding

8 *American servings*
8 *Chinese servings*

   2 *cups long grain rice*
   1 *to 1½ cups assorted fruits
    and nuts**
   4 *cups water*
¼ *cup sugar*
   6 *tablespoons lard*
   8 *tablespoons canned red
    bean paste or homemade
    red bean paste*
   1 *cup water*
   8 *tablespoons sugar*
   1 *teaspoon almond essence*
   1 *tablespoon cornstarch*
   3 *tablespoons cold water*

Wash the rice and drain.
Prepare fruits and nuts. (See
note at the end of the recipe.)
Place the rice in a heavy pan,
add 4 cups water and bring to a
boil. Reduce heat, cover and
cook over low heat for about
25 minutes or until dry and
fluffy. Let rice cool slightly and
then mix in ¼ cup sugar and
4 tablespoons lard until well
blended. Brush the inside of a
rather shallow, heatproof bowl
or dish with the remaining
melted lard, let cool and allow
to set slightly. Place fruits and
nuts in a beautiful pattern on
the bottom and sides of the dish,
pressing them lightly so they
will be embedded in the lard.
Carefully fill the dish with half
of the rice, pressing down
gently without damaging the
fruit and nut design. Cover with
a layer of bean paste, keeping
the paste within 1 to 1½ inches
from the sides. Add the
remaining rice and press down
gently so the pudding will hold
its shape when it is unmolded.
Cover with a clean cloth or foil
and steam for 1 hour. Take the
bowl out of the steaming pan
and cover with a flat serving
plate just large enough to hold
the pudding. Invert the pudding
onto the plate. Heat 1 cup
water to boiling point. Stir in
the sugar and almond essence.
Continue cooking until the
sugar has dissolved. Dissolve
the cornstarch in the water.
Add cornstarch paste to boiling
syrup and stir until thickened.
Pour sauce over pudding and
serve hot or cold.
*The original Chinese recipe
prescribes all sorts of dried or
preserved fruits and nuts which
are not obtainable in this
country. They can be substituted,
however, by your own choice of
fresh or preserved fruits and
nuts, such as, plums, raisins,
dates, candied cherries, orange
peel and other candied or
preserved fruits and nuts such
as almonds, walnuts, lotus seeds,
melon seeds etc. It is good to
have at least 8 different items
to justify the name of the
pudding. Nuts should be
blanched and halved evenly.
The fruits should be pitted
and halved or quartered, if
large. Though the lard may be
substituted by oil, lard is
preferable because the fruits
and nuts have to be arranged on
the bottom of the dish and will
stick to the surface better.
Fruits, especially candied fruits,
can be cut into half moon or
other patterns to make a
beautiful decoration.

Banquet dishes

Two soups made of ingredients that to the West are almost synonymous with Chinese food: Bird's nests and Shark's fins, (recipes page 89, 2nd and 3rd column).

Probably the most famous of them all is Peking Duck of which the crackling skin, saturated with honey is the best part, (recipe page 90, 1st column).

Shark's fin soup

Bird's nest soup

Peking doilies

Under this heading you will find a number of dishes that are fairly expensive, or require a little more skill in preparing them. These dishes are generally left to professional cooks and are served only on special occasions or at banquets. However, they are certainly not beyond the capabilities of a reasonably experienced household cook and there is a great deal of pleasure to be gained both in cooking and eating them.

6 American servings
6 Chinese servings

¼ pound dried shark's fin
2 dried Chinese mushrooms
2 thin slices fresh ginger root
½ cup fresh or canned crabmeat
8 cups chicken broth
1 tablespoon sherry
1 scallion, finely chopped
1 teaspoon cornstarch
2 tablespoons cold chicken broth

Soak the shark's fin overnight in hot water. Rinse under cold running water and remove any bones and other hard pieces. Soak mushrooms separately in hot water for about 20 minutes. Squeeze dry, remove stalks and shred caps finely. Place shark's fin in a pan and cover with plenty of cold water. Bring to a boil, reduce heat and simmer for 30 minutes. Drain and add new water and ginger. Bring to the boil again and simmer for 2½ to 3 hours. Meanwhile pick over the crabmeat, flake and remove all cartilage. Bring chicken broth to a boil and cook, uncovered until reduced to about 6 cups and very rich. Stir in the sherry. Drain shark's fin again and add to the broth together with the scallion. Bring to a boil, reduce heat and simmer, covered, for about 30 to 40 minutes or until tender. Add crabmeat and mushrooms and simmer for another 8 to 10 minutes. Meanwhile dissolve cornstarch in remaining chicken broth and stir in to thicken.

8 American servings
8 Chinese servings

4 to 5 ounces dried bird's nests
8 to 9 cups chicken broth (recipe page 19)
Breast meat of ½ chicken, skinned, boned and minced
2 tablespoons sherry
2 tablespoons water or chicken broth
2 egg whites
½ teaspoon salt
½ tablespoon cornstarch, dissolved in
2 tablespoons cold chicken broth
2 tablespoons ham-garnish (recipe page 21)

Soak the bird's nests in cold water overnight. Clean, drain and remove any remaining feathers. Place in a saucepan and cover with water. Bring to a boil and simmer for about 25 minutes. Drain. Bring the chicken broth to a boil and cook over rather high heat until reduced to slightly more than 6 cups. Add bird's nests and simmer for about 10 minutes. Mix the chicken breast with sherry and broth. Beat the egg whites for 30 seconds, add to the chicken mixture and blend well. Add the salt to the hot broth and then slowly add chicken mixture, stirring constantly. Stir cornstarch mixture in to thicken. Serve in individual bowls, topped with a little of the ham-garnish.

15 to 25 doilies

1 cup water
2 cups sifted all purpose flour
Flour
Peanut oil or sesame oil, or a combination of the 2

Bring the water to a boil and gradually add the flour, stirring with a wooden spoon until well blended. Knead the mixture on a floured board until smooth (about 10 minutes). Cover with a damp towel and let stand for 10 minutes. Form the dough into a long roll about 2 inches in diameter. Cut in ½ inch thick slices. Flatten to a ¼ inch thickness and brush one side of half the rounds with a little oil. Place 1 unoiled round on top of the oiled side of another. Dust each pair with flour and roll out to a very thin pancake, about 4½ to 5 inches in diameter. Roll from the center, turning the pancake a little after each roll to ensure a perfect round form with an even thickness. Heat an ungreased skillet or griddle over low to medium heat and bake 1 pancake at a time for about 1 minute on each side or until lightly coloured. Transfer to a platter, separate the 2 halves and keep them covered with a towel until all pancakes are ready. Peking doilies can be made in advance, kept in the refrigerator and reheated by steaming for 8 to 10 minutes. This recipe makes 15 to 25 doilies, depending on their thickness.

Peking duck

6 American servings
6 Chinese servings

1 (4 pound) duck
  Boiling water
½ to ¾ cup water
4 tablespoons honey
1 recipe Peking Doilies (see
  page 89)
18 onion brushes (see page 20)
½ cucumber (optional)
¼ to ½ cup hoisin sauce or
  plum sauce

If possible, choose a fresh duck with the neck and skin intact. Wash the duck, immerse in boiling water, lift it out again and dry thoroughly inside and out. Tie a cord around the neck and hang the bird overnight in a cool airy place to allow the skin to dry thoroughly. Dissolve the honey in the water and brush or rub the duck skin with this mixture until it is completely saturated with honey. Again hang the duck to dry completely. Place a dish under the duck to collect the drippings. Hang for 6 hours until the skin is dry and slightly hardened by the honey. Meanwhile, prepare the Peking doilies and the onion brushes. Peel the cucumber and cut in half lengthwise. Scoop out the seedy center part and cut in ⅛ to ¼ inch strips about 2½ inches long. Place the duck on a rack over a drip pan. Roast in a 350° oven without basting for about 1 to 1¼ hours or until the skin is nicely browned and crisp. With a very sharp knife, slice off the skin and cut into rectangular

pieces about 2½ inches long and 1½ inches wide or in 1½ to 2 inch squares. Carve the meat in rather thick slices to be served after the skin during the same meal. Put a doily in front of you, and on it place one or two pieces of skin. Dip an onion brush in the hoisin or plum sauce and spread a little over the skin. Put the onion brush and some cucumber strips on top. Roll up the doily and eat it with your hands. The carcass can be used in the preparation of stock.
Note: Sometimes only the skin is eaten this way and the duck meat is then used as an ingredient for other preparations.

Ta pin lo or hot pot cookery

8 to 10 American servings
8 to 10 Chinese servings

½ pound lean pork
½ pound flank steak
1 chicken breast, boned
½ pound calves' liver
½ pound lean ham
½ pound fillet of sole or
  flounder
8 to 10 small fresh oysters
8 to 10 giant shrimp, shelled
  and deveined
2 cakes bean curd
8 to 10 dried Chinese
  mushrooms, soaked 20
  minutes in hot water
¾ cup bamboo shoots
1 cup celery cabbage
8 to 10 scallions
10 to 12 cups chicken broth
1 sauce dish each of soy
  sauce, hoisin sauce, plum
  sauce, hot mustard sauce,
  vinegar, sugar
1 small bowl chopped parsley
2 tablespoons shredded fresh
  ginger root
2 tablespoons shredded
  preserved red ginger
8 to 10 small sauce dishes,
  each containing:
  2 tablespoons soy sauce,
  1 tablespoon sherry and 2
  tablespoons cornstarch,
  mixed and 1 raw egg, beaten

To set the table:
1 dinner plate
1 soup bowl
1 soup spoon
1 sauce bowl to mix sauces
2 pairs of chopsticks for
  each diner

Put pork, beef, chicken, liver, ham and sole in the freezer

compartment of the refrigerator and leave for 10 to 20 minutes or until they become firm and easier to slice very thinly. Cut meats across the grain as thinly as possible and then in 2 inch long and ¾ to 1 inch wide slices. Slice fish very thinly and then cut in 2 inch long strips. Cut oysters in half if they are not really small. Cut shrimp in 4 slices lengthwise. Cut bean curd in ¼ inch thick slices and halve each slice crosswise. Remove stems from mushrooms and cut caps into thin slices, holding the knife at a 30° angle. Cut bamboo shoots in 1/16 to ⅛ inch thick slices. Cut celery cabbage in 2 inch long strips. Put all ingredients in neat and attractive layers on individual plates. Cut scallions in ½ inch long pieces and shred lengthwise or make into onion brushes (see page 20). When using an authentic Ta pin lo, light some charcoal in a heavy, foil lined pan, bucket or other container. Burn the charcoal in an outdoor area. Put the Ta pin lo in the center of a table (preferably round formica) on an asbestos pad and surround with the ingredients, sauces and other condiments attractively arranged. Set the table by grouping a small sauce dish containing the soy, sherry and cornstarch mixture, a small sauce dish containing the beaten egg, 1 dinner plate, 1 soup bowl, 1 soup spoon, 1 sauce bowl to mix sauces and 2 pairs of chopsticks in front

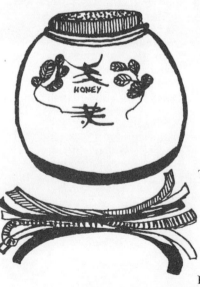

of each guest. Bring the chicken broth to a rolling boil and pour into the moat of the hot pot. Cover with a lid. When white ash has formed on the charcoal, bring the container inside and transfer the charcoal with tongs to the inside of the chimney. Add as much charcoal as needed to bring the broth to the boil again. Remove the lid from the broth and the dinner is ready for serving. Each diner puts one or more morsels of his choice in the boiling stock and cooks it to his taste. Cooking time should be short, about 1 minute for most ingredients. It is customary to start with meat and poultry and proceed to the seafood, leaving the vegetables until last, but there are no strict rules as to the order of ingredients to be cooked. The meat may be dipped in the soy, sherry and cornstarch mixture to coat before cooking. When a specific ingredient is cooked to taste, it is transferred to the diner's plate and eaten with the other pair of chopsticks. It is eaten plainly, or dipped into one of the sauces or condiments, or it may be dipped into the raw egg first to cool it slightly and give it a velvety taste before adding sauces, onions, ginger or parsley. When all the ingredients have been cooked or when diners feel that they have had enough, the soup bowl is filled with the broth, by now enriched with all the flavors of the ingredients which have been cooked in it.

The broth is drunk to conclude the meal. Parboiled noodles (see page 77) may be added to the broth to heat through for a few minutes and then be added to the soup. Also, pea starch noodles may be soaked for about 20 minutes in cold water and then added to the broth halfway through the meal. At the end of the meal, a raw egg for each diner may be poached in the bouillon, either in a ladle or in a cupped cabbage or lettuce leaf.

Ingredients

It is quite true that Chinese cooking techniques can be applied to Western ingredients. With a bottle of good soy sauce and fresh ginger root you can produce a vast number of quite satisfying and authentic dishes. But since many typical Chinese ingredients are available in supermarkets nowadays it really is worth the trouble to try them. They will certainly enhance the flavor, the color and the authenticity of your dishes. Some ingredients can easily be substituted and some can be made at home. Though cloud ear mushrooms, seaweed or sea cucumber are by no means essential in producing authentic Chinese food, when you can lay your hands on special Chinese ingredients, do not hesitate to try them. Even if the price seems high, remember that with these ingredients a little goes a long way. They are used in small quantities and most of them can be kept quite satisfactorily for a long period of time. A number of Chinese ingredients used in the recipes of this book are described here in alphabetical order.

Abalone
A mollusk with a beautiful shell that is iridescent on the inside and has a long row of little holes in it. Though available fresh in some parts of the USA (California), canned abalone is more convenient because it is already cooked and needs only brief reheating. Cooking too long makes it tough. The cooking liquid can be used in soups. Abalone can be kept for a few days in fresh water in the refrigerator. No substitute.

Bamboo shoots
The young shoots of the bamboo plant, available canned and only occasionally fresh. Whole shoots in water are the best choice. Needs only a very short cooking time but can be cooked for a longer time without losing much of its quality. Crisp and with a delicate sweet taste, they can be stored immersed in clean water in a covered jar for a few weeks in the refrigerator. Rinse bamboo shoots under cold running water before use. No substitute, though other vegetables can replace bamboo in many dishes.

Bean curd
Made from soy beans. The soy beans are made into a sort of milk from which a curd or 'cheese' is made. This is pressed into a block or into cakes. Three-inch square white cakes, about one-inch thick, are generally available. Regarded as a vegetable and an important source of protein, bean curd is very inexpensive and can be combined with almost every other ingredient. There are almost no limits to the ways in which it can be prepared. It has very little taste of its own, but easily absorbs the flavor of other ingredients and has a very pleasant texture. It only needs to be heated through, but can stand longer cooking if necessary. May be bought in single cakes, in cans, or by weight. Make sure to buy plain white bean curd, especially when buying it in cans, as many deep fried, spiced or other varieties are available in cans too. Bean curd should be handled as little as possible since it is very fragile. It is best kept immersed in water and can be stored only for two to three days at the most.

Bean sprouts
The sprouts of mung peas, the dark green husks of which are often still attached to the yellowish heads of the sprouts. This husk has to be removed which can best be done by washing the beans in water and carefully rubbing off the husks between your fingers. If the tail ends are dark and wilted, remove them too. Though it is a lot of work, it is worth doing. The fresh variety is preferable, but canned bean sprouts are a good substitute. Their taste is very good and the crispness can be restored by leaving them in ice water for half an hour. They can be kept for a few days by washing them well and storing them in the refrigerator.

Black beans, fermented
These small, black, salted soy beans have a strong salty taste. They are almost always used in combination with garlic and must be soaked for about 10–15 minutes in cold water and rinsed to remove the excess salt. They can be kept for quite a long time in a closed plastic bag or tightly capped jar.

Bird's nests
Actually the edible, gelatenous mass is produced in the saliva of a certain species of swallows which live in Southeast Asia. They are collected by daring men who climb the sides of caves, seemingly regardless of the danger of breaking their necks by falling down. After the nests have been collected, feathers, twigs and dust are removed as much as possible before packing them. The highest grade are the whole nests which resemble a small transparent cup. Broken nests or fragments are cheaper, but still very expensive. They have to be soaked overnight and afterwards have to be cleaned to remove impurities. They are rich in vitamins and protein and have a very subtle taste. Generally made into a soup to be served at banquet dinners or on very special occasions. Sold by weight, packed in a paper box. If kept tightly wrapped they can be stored for quite a long time. No substitute.

Bitter lemon
Also called balsam pear, karela or bitter gourd, it is the elongated, wrinkled green fruit of a tropical plant; sold in cans and occasionally fresh. Has a distinctive but not unpleasant bitter flavor. It is parboiled to get rid of excess bitterness. Can be kept in the refrigerator in a perforated plastic bag for about five to seven days. Can be substituted by cucumber. Before use, the seedy, spongy inner part has to be removed.

Brown bean sauce
An aromatic, thick, fermented sauce made of yellow-brown beans. Used as a flavoring, it is cooked with other ingredients like fish, beef, bean curd etc. Japanese aka-miso is a good substitute. Kept in a tightly covered jar in the refrigerator, it keeps for a very long time.

Celery cabbage
Also called Chinese lettuce or napa, it is a delicious crisp vegetable with long leaves that are whiteish and firm in the stemlike centerpart and light green and fringed at the sides and top. The leaves are tightly packed together. Ideal for stir fried dishes and requires only a short cooking time. Can be kept in a perforated plastic bag in the refrigerator for a few days. Other crisp vegetables can be substituted.

Chinese cabbage
Similar to celery cabbage, but the leaves are darker and are not as tightly cropped. Combines very well with other ingredients and is very versatile. Storing is the same as with celery cabbage. Other crisp vegetables can be substituted.

Chinese dried mushrooms
Dried mushrooms of a dark brown color with rather large caps. They have to be soaked in hot water, and then have a distinctive, somewhat meaty flavor. Very versatile, frequently used with almost all other ingredients, and suitable for most cooking techniques. Sold

by weight. Rather expensive, but only used sparingly. Essential ingredient. Can be substituted by other dried mushrooms.

Chinese sausages
Chinese pork sausages, about 4 to 6 inches long and ½ to ¾ inch in diameter, have a sweet taste and combine very well with chicken, rice, omelettes and other bland food. They are steamed with other ingredients or steamed first and then stir fried with other ingredients. Often tied together as a pair. Available in cans and occasionally fresh. Can be washed before use. If wrapped in foil they can be kept in the refrigerator or in the freezer for months. Smoked uncooked ham, chopped with some pork fat, marinated in a little sherry and sugar and then steamed for about 20 minutes, may serve as a substitute in some cases.

Chinese parsley
Also called cilantro. These are fresh coriander leaves. This herb looks very much like parsley but has a quite different and much stronger taste. Is used instead of parsley by the Chinese. Should be used in smaller quantities than parsley. Store like parsley.

Five spice powder
A brown powdered mixture of star anise, cloves, cinnamon, anise pepper and fennel. Used sparingly in red simmered and roasted meat and poultry dishes. Sold in tins or by weight. Allspice can be substituted.

Ginger root, fresh
A fibrous, irregularly shaped tubular root of a tropical plant. Yellowish ivory colored inside with a light brown smooth skin, it is extensively used minced, shredded or sliced in a vast number of dishes. The part which lies directly under the stem is the youngest and most delicate part, it has no or very few fibers. Ginger root can be kept alive and even growing in a pot covered with earth and sand and given water regularly. Take out when needed, slice off what is necessary and return the rest. Ginger root should be lightly scraped, not peeled. It is also possible to keep fresh ginger root (washed, scraped and cut into pieces) in sherry in a tightly capped jar in the refrigerator. Never use dried or powdered ginger as a substitute in Chinese cooking. If the fresh root is not available, use well washed, preserved ginger.

Glutinous rice
Very white in color, short grained and sticky when cooked. Used sometimes to stuff poultry, or as a coating for meat balls and in other, often sweet, dishes. Wash before use. When steamed as a coating for meat balls, it should have a preliminary soaking. No substitute.

Hoisin sauce
Comes under many different names. A sweet and spicy, reddish-brown sauce. Used to marinate roast meats or poultry, it is often combined with other

sauces as a dip, etc. Made from soy beans. Sold generally in cans or bottles. If kept in a tightly capped jar, it can be stored in the refrigerator for many months. No substitute.

Kumquats

A very small fruit of the Fortunella genus, closely related to the citrus family. Looks like a miniature orange and has a strong orange flavor. Available in cans, preserved in syrup. Occasionally fresh. It is eaten whole. Often combined with other fruits. No substitute.

Lychees

Also spelled litchee or litchi, though of Chinese origin, is now grown in other subtropical areas also in the USA. Has a crimson pink skin and translucent silky white, jellylike flesh around a big brown seed. Has a very special subtle flavor. Available in cans and occasionally fresh.
Sometimes available dried; the pulp is then like a raisin and very sweet. Lychees can be used with other fruits as a dessert. Also used sometimes with poultry, shrimp and pork.

Longans

Similar to lychees, but smaller and with a pale brown skin. Has the same pulpy flesh and subtle flavor. Comes mainly in cans. Also sold dried. Used in some soups. No substitute.

Monosodium glutamate (Ve-tsin)

A very fine white powder, with no flavor of its own. Used to enhance the flavor of other ingredients. Opinions differ greatly on the subject of whether or not it should be used. If good and fresh ingredients are used and prepared in the correct way, it will not be missed at all. If used, it should be used only sparingly. No substitute.

Noodles

Threadlike pasta in various lengths, widths and thicknesses and made of different materials, mostly flour. Most common types are egg noodles and rice noodles.

Egg noodles

Made of hard wheat flour and eggs. Comes in different shapes and is sold dried packed in cellophane, and sometimes fresh in Chinese shops. The dried variety comes in nests; in spaghetti-like bunches, or in cakes. Noodles should be cooked to a consistency that Italians call 'al dente', which means that they should be tender but still firm. Can be used parboiled, stir fried, braised or in soups.

Rice noodles

Made of rice flour. Long, opaque white, brittle threads. Always sold dried. Can be used like egg noodles for cooked and stir fried dishes. Can also be deep fried, which makes them puff up and become very crisp. In this way they are mainly used as a garnish.

Oyster sauce

A rich velvety sauce made of oysters, their cooking liquid and soy sauce. Thick and greyish dark brown. It is often used in seafood dishes, but also blends well with all meats and poultry and with bean curd and vegetables. Very good flavor. Sold in bottles or canned. A fair substitute can be made at home (recipe see page 82). Use sparingly. Store in a tightly covered jar. Will keep for some months.

Plum sauce

Amber colored sauce, resemblying a chutney in consistency. Made from plums, other fruits, hot pepper, vinegar and sugar. Has a spicy and hot sweet-sour flavor. Used almost exclusively as a dip sauce with roast meats, poultry, cold meats, egg rolls etc. A fair substitute can be made at home (see recipe on page 83). Store in a tightly covered jar. Will keep for months.

Rice

Long grain rice, or Patna rice is most commonly used in Chinese cooking. Sometimes also the short grain variety is used, which is somewhat softer and not quite as suitable for use in fried rice dishes. Both types can be boiled or steamed. Store in a dry place.

Sesame oil

Oil extracted from sesame seed. Has a very strong, nutty flavor of its own and is therefore almost exclusively used as a flavoring in soups, with stir fried dishes, etc. Is sold in bottles.

Needs no special care in storing. The color can vary from almost transparent to a dark brown. No substitute.

Shark's fins

Very expensive, transparent, slightly curled, dried delicacy. It is the threadlike cartilage of the shark's fin, which has been dried. Has a subtle flavor. Must be soaked overnight and can then be used in soups, in stir fried dishes or to stuff chicken. (Combines well also with eggs and crab.) Sold by weight, generally packed in a box or a cellophane wrapper. Will keep for a long time when kept in the wrapper. No substitute.

Shrimp

Shrimp are used very frequently in Chinese cooking, either alone or combined with other seafood, meats (especially pork) and vegetables. They can be deep fried, stir fried or steamed. The Chinese use all sorts of shrimp, from the giant or jumbo shrimp to the miniature or baby shrimp. This baby shrimp is also sold in a dried variety. The latter is often used to enhance the flavor of vegetables or used in soups. Fresh or frozen baby shrimp are used stir fried or as a popular filling ingredient for eggrolls. For most stir fried dishes, small or medium sized shrimp are the best choice, but for deep frying the giant shrimp is chosen, sometimes 'butterflied', that is cut open lengthwise. For stir fried dishes large shrimp can be cut in half or into pieces.

Cooking time is important with shrimp since too long a cooking period makes them tough. Shrimp balls are preferably made from large shrimp. Before use, the black vein of the shrimp should be removed.

Soy sauce

Often referred to as the most important ingredient in Chinese cooking, this brown sauce made of soy beans and other ingredients indeed enhances the flavor of almost every dish whether meat, poultry, seafood or vegetables. It is sold in many grades, many colors and thicknesses. Three main types are usually specified. Light soy (called Sang Chan) is most widely used in cooking. Dark soy, (to which caramel is added) is added to intensify the taste and color of a dish, or used on the table. Heavy soy (Yee Yau or See Yow), which is made from molasses, is viscous and bittersweet. It is used very sparingly to add color rather than taste. Soy sauces imported from China are the best because they have been matured and aged slowly and, though they are somewhat more expensive, they are very much worth the extra money. No substitute.

Star anise

Star shaped seed cluster containing shiny brown seeds. Not related to the well-known anise seed, but to the magnolia family. Used to flavor red simmered dishes. Sold by weight. Anise seed can be substituted.

Tangerine peel

The dried skin of tangerines, a favorite flavoring for duck, but also used with meats (especially red simmered dishes), in some soups and sometimes in congee. Only a small piece is used at a time. High prices are paid for tangerine peel that has been left to age for several decades to improve the flavor. Sold by weight. Usually soaked in water. for about 20 to 30 minutes. No substitutes.

Tea melon

Also called preserved cucumber. A small melon that resembles a miniature cucumber. The color is a greenish brown or dark green. It is sold canned, preserved in honey. Sometimes used in steamed meat or fish dishes, also as an ingredient in noodle dishes. Can be kept in the refrigerator in a tightly capped jar for months. No substitute.

Water chestnuts

The squat, dark brown tubes of an aquatic plant that grows in marshes in East Asia. When peeled that are white and crisp and have a fresh, sweet taste. Often used together with bamboo in stir fried dishes. Blends with almost all other ingredients. Available canned and occasionally fresh. Can be stored immersed in fresh water for about 2 to 3 weeks, in a tightly capped jar. Change the water every 2 or 3 days. No substitute.

Conversion tables

Liquid measures

American
standard cup

metric equivalent
(approximately)

1 cup = $\frac{1}{2}$ pint	= 8 fl. oz. (fluid ounce)	= 2,37 dl (deciliter)
1 tbs. (tablespoon) = $\frac{1}{2}$ fl. oz.		= 1,5 cl (centiliter)
1 tsp. (teaspoon) = $\frac{1}{6}$ fl. oz.		= 0,5 cl
1 pint	= 16 fl. oz.	= 4,73 dl
1 quart = 2 pints	= 32 fl. oz.	= 9,46 dl

British
standard cup

metric equivalent
(approximately)

1 cup = $\frac{1}{2}$ pint	= 10 fl. oz.	= 2,84 dl
1 tbs	= 0.55 fl. oz.	= 1,7 cl
1 tsp.	= $\frac{1}{5}$ fl. oz.	= 0,6 cl
1 pint	= 20 fl. oz.	= 5,7 dl
1 quart = 2 pints	= 40 fl. oz.	= 1,1 l (liter)

1 cup = 16 tablespoons
1 tablespoon = 3 teaspoons

1 liter = 10 deciliter = 100 centiliter

Oven temperatures

Centigrade	Fahrenheit	
up to 105° C	up to 225° F	cool
105–135° C	225–275° F	very slow
135–160° C	275–325° F	slow
175–190° C	350–375° F	moderate
215–230° C	400–450° F	hot
230–260° C	450–500° F	very hot
260° C	500° F	extremely hot

Solid measures

American/British

metric equivalent
(approximately)

1 lb. (pound)	= 16 oz. (ounces)	= 453 g (gram)
	1 oz.	= 28 g
2.2 lbs.		= 1000 g = 1 kg (kilogram)
	$3\frac{1}{2}$ oz.	= 100 g

Alphabetical index

Index by type of dish

DANCE
ANATOMY

Jacqui Greene Haas

Human Kinetics

Library of Congress Cataloging-in-Publication Data

Haas, Jacqui Greene, 1958-
 Dance anatomy / Jacqui Greene Haas.
  p. cm.
 ISBN-13: 978-0-7360-8193-1 (soft cover)
 ISBN-10: 0-7360-8193-3 (soft cover)
 1. Dance--Physiological aspects. I. Title.
 RC1220.D35H33 2010
 612'.044--dc22

                                        2009045722

 ISBN-10: 0-7360-8193-3 (print)
 ISBN-13: 978-0-7360-8193-1 (print)

This publication is written and published to provide accurate and authoritative information relevant to the subject matter presented. It is published and sold with the understanding that the author and publisher are not engaged in rendering legal, medical, or other professional services by reason of their authorship or publication of this work. If medical or other expert assistance is required, the services of a competent professional person should be sought.

Acquisitions Editors: Judy Patterson Wright, PhD, Laurel Plotzke Garcia; **Developmental Editors:** Amanda Eastin-Allen, Cynthia McEntire; **Assistant Editor:** Laura Podeschi; **Copyeditor:** Jan Feeney; **Permission Manager:** Martha Gullo; **Graphic Designer:** Fred Starbird; **Graphic Artist:** Kim McFarland; **Cover Designer:** Keith Blomberg; **Photographer (for illustration references):** Peter Mueller; **Photo Manager:** Neil Bernstein; **Visual Production Assistant:** Joyce Brumfield; **Art Manager:** Kelly Hendren; **Associate Art Manager:** Alan L. Wilborn; **Illustrator (cover):** Jennifer Gibas; **Illustrators (interior):** Fran Milner, Jennifer Gibas; **Printer:** Courier Corporation

Human Kinetics books are available at special discounts for bulk purchase. Special editions or book excerpts can also be created to specification. For details, contact the Special Sales Manager at Human Kinetics.

Printed in the United States of America   10   9   8   7   6   5   4   3   2

The papers in this book were manufactured using responsible forestry methods.

Human Kinetics
Web site: www.HumanKinetics.com

United States: Human Kinetics
P.O. Box 5076
Champaign, IL 61825-5076
800-747-4457
e-mail: humank@hkusa.com

Canada: Human Kinetics
475 Devonshire Road Unit 100
Windsor, ON N8Y 2L5
800-465-7301 (in Canada only)
e-mail: info@hkcanada.com

Europe: Human Kinetics
107 Bradford Road
Stanningley
Leeds LS28 6AT, United Kingdom
+44 (0) 113 255 5665
e-mail: hk@hkeurope.com

Australia: Human Kinetics
57A Price Avenue
Lower Mitcham, South Australia 5062
08 8372 0999
e-mail: info@hkaustralia.com

New Zealand: Human Kinetics
P.O. Box 80
Torrens Park, South Australia 5062
0800 222 062
e-mail: info@hknewzealand.com

E4776

CONTENTS